Your Retirement Highway

HOW TO SET YOUR FINANCES ON CRUISE CONTROL

By Ken and Lori Heise

Heise Advisory Group

St. Louis, Missouri

Ken and Lori Heise/Heise Advisory Group
12444 Powerscourt Drive, Suite 235
St. Louis, MO 63131
www.heiseadvisorygroup.com

Book Layout ©2013 BookDesignTemplates.com

Your Retirement Highway/ Ken and Lori Heise. —1st ed.
ISBN 978-1728668314

Contents

We want to dedicate our book to our family for all the love and support that they have given us throughout this growing process. We also want to thank all of our wonderful clients for putting their faith and trust in us and for believing that we could truly help them to achieve their retirement goals.

Foreword

By **Whitey Herzog**

Ken and Lori Heise are great Cardinal fans, and it's a pleasure to introduce their book. They are also great supporters of the game of baseball, and I have thoroughly enjoyed being with them at some of the pre-game and post-game events they sponsor at the stadium, along with radio station KMOX. When they asked me to write a foreword to their book, I readily agreed. I also told them that what I know about finance is not going to impress anybody. I'm a baseball guy. What I know about money management can boil down to five words, "Let the professionals handle it."

When I first started playing professionally with the New York Yankees organization in the 1950s, it sure wasn't for the money. I got a $1,500 signing bonus and $150 per month. People think I'm joking when I tell them this, but I never made more than $18,000 per year playing baseball. During the off-season I worked at a bakery, a brewery and a brick and pipe company to support Mary Lou and the kids. We lived in a little travel trailer we dragged from town to town until 1958. The only way I could afford to build a house was to build it myself. I took some technical school courses to learn how and built it during the off-season.

My first major league gig was with the Washington Senators. The New York Yankees signed me because I was a left-handed hitter and a left-handed thrower, but I had trouble hitting the curveball, so they traded me to the Senators in 1956. It was the big leagues, but it surely wasn't the big bucks.

Television was just coming of age in the 1950s when I began playing, and few games were televised. There were only three TV cameras. They were huge, too. They put them on the Mezzanine level of the stadium. Those old black and white cameras were dinosaurs compared to the equipment they use today. They could swivel but had no zoom capability. All you got at home was a boring wide-angle view of the field. No close-ups. No graphics. The game announcer had one microphone and there was another one for the crowd noise, but that was it. Cave-man stuff compared to today. But people watched it. In fact, it was the revenue from the television networks that really started to boost players' salaries.

When Mickey Mantle broke into the big leagues in 1951, he was earning only $7,500 per year. The year he won the American League Most Valuable Player award in 1956 he earned a whopping $33,000. People don't believe me when I tell them that in 1968, the final year of his career, Mantle was making only $100,000 per year.

The best thing that came from my association with the Yankee organization was getting to know Yankee manager Casey Stengel. I loved the guy and for some reason, he liked me. I learned more about the game of baseball just hanging around Casey than I could ever put in a book. He was something else.

I first met Casey in 1954. I had just left military service after the Korean War ended, and the Yankees had invited me to their rookie camp. He was in his 60s and I thought that was pretty old at the time. But he had the wisdom and intelligence not to judge a player by his stats. Casey looked for potential and, if it was there, he found it. He had a way of spotting what a player could do and concentrating on that, building on it. He had a special way of communicating with players. It was like he had his own language.

What he said would echo in your brain and sometimes what he meant would hit me hours or even days later.

We did become good friends, and the press has always made a big deal about it. I think one of the reasons why he took a liking to me was because of a misimpression he had that I never did clear up. He had played with a fellow by the name of Bud Herzog, and I believe to this day that Casey thought I was his grandson. I never told him any different, either. He would say, "How is Granddad?" I'd say, "Oh, he's great."

For some reason, Casey was sure that I was going to be a manager. When somebody of his caliber believes in you, it's only natural for a little bit of that confidence to rub off. So, after a while, I started believing it myself. I hadn't done anything in my life, but maybe I could do this.

One day we were talking over a couple of sodas after a game, and he said, "If you're going to be a manager, you've got to learn how to handle the press. You're going to get interviewed a lot by the TV networks. Always ask the guy who is interviewing you how much time he has and how many questions he is going to ask you."

"Why do you do that?" I asked.

"Because when he says he is going to interview you for 15 minutes and has three questions, you talk for 15 minutes answering his first question and then you don't have to worry about the other two."

Casey gave me some of the best advice I ever got about managing baseball teams.

"Don't try to do it all yourself," he told me. "Hire good coaches … and don't worry about them taking your job. If you screw up you'll get fired anyway." A lot of people thought he was a little eccentric, and they were wrong about that. He was a **lot** eccentric. But he was a great manager and a great guy and I miss him.

As a player, I did okay, but I wasn't great. Like I always say, baseball has been good to me, especially since I quit trying to play it. I am grateful to have had the opportunity to contribute what I have to the game — a lot of blood and sweat, but few tears. I have played for and managed a lot of teams and have enjoyed every minute of it.

I wouldn't take anything for the privilege and honor it has been to be involved with the St. Louis Cardinals organization. They are the very best in baseball as far as I'm concerned. When Gussie Busch hired me to manage the Cards in 1980, I knew I had found a good place to try some theories that I thought would work, and I was fortunate to have talented people around me that were willing to help me implement them. But I had no idea we would be as successful as we were. We won the 1982 World Series and had two more shots at it in 1985 and 1987.

It was a thrill for me personally to be inducted into the Baseball Hall of Fame on July 25, 2010. I don't think a lot of people knew my real name wasn't "Whitey" until then. People sometimes ask me how I got the nickname "Whitey." I ask them which they would rather be called: "Whitey" or "Dorrel Norman Elvert." The latter is how it is displayed on my plaque in Cooperstown. I was happy to see the two nicknames by which I came to be known, "Whitey" and "The White Rat," listed there as well. The real story behind those nicknames had to do with my resemblance to Yankee pitcher Bob Kuzava. We both had crewcuts and white hair. Kuzava was known as "The Rat." I hit a grand slam home run in a game with the Milwaukee Braves one year, and the sportscaster said, "The *white rat* nails one." That's how it came out in the paper the next day, and the name stuck. Later it was shortened to "Whitey."

A lot of fuss has been made in the press about "Whitey Ball," as the press described our style of play when I was managing the Cardinals the year we won the World Series in 1982. We didn't have a lot of power hitters, so it was no genius on my part; we just used what we had. We had speed on the base path and some excellent defensive skills. We could hit good line drives, too. And we had a secret weapon — the AstroTurf at Busch Memorial Stadium, which gave the other team some crazy bounces when the ball was hit at sharp angles. We would get a run or a walk, a stolen base or two, a sacrifice bunt and maybe a sacrifice fly — a lot of little successes that would translate into a lead. In 1982, our entire team only hit 67 home runs all season. The team we beat in the World Series, the Milwaukee Brewers, had hit 216 home runs that year. When they ripped up the artificial turf in 1995 and replaced it with grass, it was like seeing an old friend go.

A lot of good things have come my way over my baseball career, not the least of which was the honor of having my jersey, number 24, retired by the Cardinals in 2010 and being inducted into the St. Louis Cardinals Hall of Fame Museum on August 16, 2014. I said blood, sweat and tears earlier. Most all of the tears have been the good kind. The kind you shed when you are over-the-top happy and proud. That's the way it feels to be honored by peers you respect and fans you love, and I have had a lot of that come my way — more than I deserve, perhaps, but I appreciate every bit of it.

Someone asked me once why I made a career out of baseball, and I remember telling them jokingly that it sure beat digging ditches in New Athens, Illinois, where I was born. I like what Ty Cobb said about baseball and money in 1909: "The great trouble with baseball today is that most of the players are in the game for the money." He said those words at a time when average annual salaries were less than $5,000. When he said that, the great Ty Cobb was earning $9,000 a year. Even though Cobb's 1909 salary is the equivalent of $200,000 today, that's a drop in the bucket to the $3.3 million average player salary today.

As I said in the beginning, I know little about managing money, but I do know a lot about people. I am truly grateful for all the good people it has been, and still is, my privilege to work with throughout the years. I would not be where I am without many friends and fans who have given me their support and encouragement along the way. I am proud to count Ken and Lori Heise among that number, and I know you will enjoy reading their book.

Whitey Herzog is not a client of Heise Advisory Group nor was he remunerated for his contributions to this book.

Ken and Lori Heise with Whitey Herzog,
supporting the Cardinals at Busch Stadium.

Preface

Retirement should be that time in your life when you get to get up every morning and celebrate the sunrise. At last, the "Golden Years" — when you can do whatever it is that you want to do. Do nothing if you want to, or everything! It's up to you. Retirement is the time you've dreamed of all your working life, and now it's finally here. You can wave goodbye to the office, or wherever and whatever your workplace consists of, and strike out to achieve your dream and follow your heart. As a husband and wife retirement advisory team, we believe retirement is not the end of the trail; it's the beginning of a new and exciting journey for the *rest* of your lives

Oh yes, while you are waving goodbye to things, you are waving goodbye to your paycheck. The idea of cutting that umbilical link that represents financial security is enough to make some people break out in hives. Have I saved enough? What if something happens? What if I get sick or injured? They say we are living longer; what if I run out of money in retirement? I don't want to be a burden on my family. Where can I invest my money to keep it working for me without taking on too much *risk* or incurring too many fees? I need to keep my money working for me in retirement; where can I invest it? What happens if I take on too much risk? Those are all good questions, and we will talk about each of them in this book.

One of our greatest privileges as advisors is to help people achieve their retirement dreams, whatever they are. We focus on helping people in or near retirement create their *Retirement*

Roadmap Review®, a strategy to hopefully get them from where they are to where they want to be. It means that we like to help people achieve not only their financial goals, but their personal goals as well. We consider it our mission to help people be who they want to be, do what they want to do and go where they want to go in retirement.

For example, one couple we met with recently told us of a passion they have had for years: visiting the Holy Land. "We have been collecting brochures on the Middle East, Jerusalem and the Greek islands for years," the wife told us. "We want to put our bare feet in the water of both the Jordan River and the Dead Sea and visit some of the places in the Bible."

Another couple said their idea of retirement is to stay at home and spend time with family. "We have a beautiful place out in the country that we have worked hard all of our lives to own and maintain," they told us. "It's not a real farm but we have goats and ducks and horses and there are riding trails nearby. We have designed it to be a regular grandkid magnet! We can't think of anything better than to spend time with them and be part of their lives growing up."

Another couple we know call themselves "ex-hippies." You would never know it from the looks of them today. He is a successful businessman and she just retired after 35 years as a high school teacher. They have a motor home and plan to travel across the country visiting each national park and many of the state parks.

As the saying goes, different strokes for different folks.

For us, retirement isn't here yet, but when it comes, our journey will be just that: a road trip — or ten — on our "his and hers" Harley-Davidson motorcycles. We started riding together in 2005. Why ride? We love the outdoors and traveling. There are just so many places we haven't been to and there is nothing quite like the communication with the road experienced when it's just

you and your bike. The sense of adventure and freedom has a lot to do with it, too. Why Harleys? No other motorcycle we know of has the same rumbling sound. There is something physically resonant about it. The Harley-Davidson people must have it patented, because it is as distinct as the people who ride them. We like to take long rides together and just take our time enjoying the scenery. We have ridden to the top of a volcano in Maui (on rented Harleys, of course), coursed and crossed both the Rockies and the Smoky Mountains, and cruised the strip in Las Vegas. We cannot decide which we love more, the Blue Ridge Parkway in the East or the Beartooth Highway in the West.

Don't be surprised if you encounter the occasional reference to cycling and our riding experiences as you continue reading. Our three passions in life are our family, retirement education and motorcycle riding. Sometimes the three things overlap when we speak and teach. For instance, just as we help families develop their *Retirement Roadmap Review*®, we like to think of each path as a person's Retirement Highway. There might be roadblocks or detours, but ultimately, we want to help people keep their finances on cruise control as much as possible.

This book will cover some pretty complex topics that we will try our best not to make more complicated. One of the reasons we chose to write this book is that we wished to put into permanent format — one that could be referenced time and again — some of the concepts about investing and retirement income planning that we deem valuable. We feel these ideas and strategies can make a huge difference in whether you realize your dreams or are forced to forfeit them in the wake of unpleasant financial reality.

Some of these concepts may be new to you, but please don't discount them because of that. Putting it plainly, there is a lot of bogus financial advice out there — most of it given by salespeople with financial products to sell. That's not what you will find here. We have nothing to sell, no axe to grind, no agenda to fill and no ulterior motives at all in what we say. Our passion is education and communication. If you are a retiree, or about to become one, you need to know your options so you can make wise and prudent decisions. We intend to pull the curtain back and shine the light of truth on some ideas that may have been in place for a long time, but simply do not work any longer in today's economy.

The Heise Advisory Group annual holiday party.

CHAPTER 1

It's All about the Journey

"Retirement is also the beginning of a journey of self-discovery. So go ahead, and rediscover yourself. Life holds a lot in store when you have the time to explore its full potential." ~ Author unknown

Some people view retirement as a destination, the end of the trail. Their plan is to work hard for a certain number of years with the goal of leaving the working life behind and entering a more relaxed lifestyle. Our contention that retirement is a journey comes from what we observe about those who are retiring these days as opposed to retirement as it was defined a few decades ago. Now that we are living longer and 60 is the new 40, gone are the days when people associated the word retirement with idleness. The vision of Ma and Pa on the front porch in matching rocking chairs is being replaced by hip, smartly dressed seniors enjoying an active life skiing, playing tennis or golf, sailing, or even riding his-and-hers Harley Davidsons.

It used to be that workers could expect to put in their three or four decades of service with one company and get a gold watch and a pension. Retirement was expected to be brief — certainly not longer than 20 years — and retirees expected to pare down their lifestyle to match their meager resources. The financial vision of retirement has changed. The new retirees are baby boomers — a generation that grew up expecting the good things in life as a matter of course. Instead of the "end-of-the-trail" mentality, this new crop of retirees knows that this is *their* time and life has just begun.

Living Longer

When Social Security was first introduced in 1935, the retirement age was 65 and so was the average lifespan. Whether you credit advances in medical science, healthier lifestyles, or the fact that fewer people use tobacco, the fact is that average life expectancy is on the rise. Men who reach age 65 are projected to live another 18 years, and for women age 65, they should be planning to live at least another 20. One 2016 study estimated that if a couple lives to 65 there is a 25 percent chance that one of them will live to the age of 98.[1]

The United States currently has the greatest number of individuals known to have lived to the age of 100, with 53,364 centenarians according to the 2010 Census. The 1980 census recorded only 32,194 individuals who had lived a century or longer...that's a 65.8 percent increase. Many new retirees can look forward to 30 years or more of retirement. It is estimated that over the next 40 years the number of people aged over 65 will almost triple, from 2.8 million today to around 7.2 million in 2047

---

[1] Robert Powell. USA Today. Oct. 5, 2016. "For your retirement planning, count on living until age 95."
https://www.usatoday.com/story/money/columnist/powell/2016/10/05/life-expectancy-actuaries-live-die-retire-retirement/89407296/.

— that's from around 13 percent of the population to over 25 percent. [2]

Reshaping Retirement

Some say even the **word** retirement, which means to withdraw or shrink back, is a bit of a misnomer. Perhaps the lexicographers should come up with a new word. How about changing it to *"advance?"*

Instead of, "Do you plan to **retire?**" how about, "Do you plan to **advance** when you turn 65?" That has a nice ring to it, don't you think? It certainly seems to reflect more accurately what is happening these days. By some estimates, there are 10,000 baby boomers (born between 1946 and 1964) retiring every day and they're not withdrawing from anything. They are moving on. They view longevity as a bonus to explore new options, pursue old dreams and live life to the fullest, expanding their social networks and pursuing second careers.

Times were when seniors were the most computer illiterate segment of the population. No more. Grandparents have discovered that FaceTime, Skype and texting are fast becoming the only ways of keeping up with their grandchildren and it is unusual to find a senior citizen who doesn't have an email address.

The Downside

All that is good news, right? Yes and no. There are some nagging "what ifs" out there that tend to darken the horizon for many seniors. The combination of increased longevity, changing

---

[2] Emily Brandon. US News. Jan. 7, 2013. "What People Who Live to 100 Have in Common." https://money.usnews.com/money/retirement/articles/2013/01/07/what-people-who-live-to-100-have-in-common.

demographics and rising expectations is creating new challenges for investors to ensure their retirement savings last the distance. Now that the first wave of baby boomers has officially reached retirement age, some are finding they aren't prepared for it. The 2008 market crash and the recession that followed it hasn't done much to brighten their outlook. In fact, in August 2017, a piece in the Washington Post titled "The job market just recovered from the recession" declared all economic metrics indicated nationwide recovery... except for the emotional and mental effects.[3] Many retirees delayed retirement because of those turbulent times or settled for a diminished retirement. Coupled with the ever-present realities of rising health care costs or long-term care, not to mention taxes and inflation uncertainties... it's no wonder retirement and severing yourself from a steady paycheck is an unnerving prospect.

Another bubble-popper has been the unexpected development of having to care for aging parents and returning adult children whose marriages didn't work out. There is even a name for those who have to cope with these unplanned responsibilities: the sandwich generation.

Planning Is Everything
"Get your motor runnin'
Head out on the highway
Looking for adventure
In whatever comes our way"
— Born to Be Wild, Steppenwolf, 1971

---

[3] Ana Swanson. The Washington Post. Aug. 4, 2017. "The job market just recovered from the recession. Men and white people haven't."
https://www.washingtonpost.com/news/wonk/wp/2017/08/04/the-job-market-just-recovered-from-the-recession-men-and-white-people-havent/?utm_term=.e1def100f5e3.

When we take off "looking for adventure" on a cross-country motorcycle trip, we pack our saddlebags very carefully: Rain gear, extra clothing in case of cold weather, flashlights, spare batteries. You never know what will happen so it's best to be prepared. The Rocky Mountains can be beautiful to ride through, but they can produce all the "adventure" you could wish for. One summer we left our starting point in short sleeves and before we got to Jackson Hole, Wyoming at 1 a.m. we had on every stitch of clothing we had packed plus heavy rain gear over our leathers.

Some things you just can't predict. Take for example the electrical problem we had with one of our bikes that gave us the "opportunity to relax" in Boise, Idaho for a few days. That stopover wasn't on our itinerary!

Then there was the monsoon combined with gale force winds we encountered while riding into Nashville, Tennessee on Interstate 40. We were covered from head to toe in our black and silver rain gear and thankful for every inch of reflective tape that came with it.

The point is, since you can't predict the unpredictable, the next best thing is to be as prepared as possible for it. And that takes planning. Sadly, most Americans spend more time planning the details of their vacation than they do their financial futures. When we have an opportunity to speak to young people about their finances, we stress the importance of setting up an emergency fund for unexpected life events that can put a sudden strain on their cash flow. What kind of things? Losing a job is one. A sudden sickness or injury or a death in the family can put a strain on cash reserves. Let's face it; life happens. Roofs fail, cars break down, and babies are born. How much should you have in your emergency fund? We recommend you keep at least six to nine months' worth of living expenses in the bank. The money should be instantly accessible, or liquid, and safe from risk of loss.

Of course, senior citizens are more vulnerable to life's unexpected events than are younger people. You have probably worked hard all your life. Hopefully you have something to show for it. Hopefully you have a healthier bank account than someone just starting out. Hopefully you have some assets set aside for your retirement — a nest egg for the golden years. But a poor investing decision or money management choice made at a critical time can wipe out decades of diligent saving. That's what happened to millions of Americans on the verge of retirement in 2008. Generally speaking, the older you are, the more is at stake.

Enjoying the Journey

The Retirement Highway is supposed to be all about being with the people you love and going where you want to go and doing what you want to do when you want to do it. But if you have to worry about what's happening in Washington or Wall Street, or if you find yourself pacing the floor at night anxious about the money in your investment account, it's not a pleasant way to spend your golden years. As motivational speaker and humorist Zig Ziglar said, "Having money isn't everything, but it ranks right up there with oxygen on the gotta have it scale." No, having an adequate supply of money doesn't necessarily define a happy retirement journey, but not having enough can certainly define an unhappy one — which is what we would like to help you avoid.

Ken and Lori Heise, 2006, taking a photo break
during a Harley ride through Sedona, Arizona.

CHAPTER 2

Know Where You
Are Financially

"A good financial plan is a road map that shows us exactly how the choices we make today will affect our future." ~ Alexa von Tobel

How important is it to know where you are?

From where we live on the outskirts of St. Louis, it's only a short hop to the West County Center shopping mall. It may not be the biggest mall in the country, but it seems plenty big to us. You can find just about anything you are looking for in the place but it's easy to get lost there. What helps me find my way is that there is a JCPenney® on one end and a Macy's on the other end and a very handy map at an information kiosk on the ground floor in between. If you are looking for a particular store and you can find your way to the information stand, you can find the store you're looking for easily enough. In the center of the map there is a red dot that says, *"YOU ARE HERE."*

When we take our bikes on road trips that involve interstate highways, we sometimes stop at the rest areas to stretch our legs. Our favorites are the ones at the state lines. They seem to have much more to offer. "Welcome to Georgia" read the sign of one

9

such service plaza we pulled into as we were heading for Atlanta after leaving Chattanooga, Tennessee. It was one of the nicer welcome stations we had seen, complete with an official welcome person and free maps. In the center of the plaza was a gigantic map of Georgia encased in glass. In the center of the map was a large red arrow that announced, *"YOU ARE HERE."*

What did we do before the days of the GPS (Global Positioning System)? A pleasant voice tells you to turn left, turn right, and even do a U-turn if you make a mistake. So common is the use of GPS anymore that it's almost hard to imagine life without it. Most smart phones these days have built in directional capabilities based on either GPS or a similar kind of triangulation technology. But whether you are lost in a mall or traveling the highways, the process of getting to where you want to go starts with first determining where you are.

It is the same with investing. We are all at a *"YOU ARE HERE"* point on a financial timeline of sorts. Each place or slot along that timeline calls for different money usage philosophy and a different investing strategy. How you view money and investing when you are 30, for example, will not be (or shouldn't be) the way you will view money and investing when you are 60.

Our financial timeline has two distinct phases:
- Accumulation
- Preservation and Distribution

Experiment with a Tape Measure

Perhaps we can illustrate this with an ordinary carpenter's tape measure. Most every house has one of these. Our house had three — two in the garage and one in a kitchen cabinet drawer that is a catch-all for everything from recipes to lids with absentee containers. The measure we used was a cassette with a retractable metal "tape" made by Lufkin and could measure up to 25 feet.

These are handy gadgets. The inches are prominently marked on the tape, which is useful for our purposes, because we are going to let the inches stand for the years of our lives.

0-21 inches: We will call these the **preparatory** years. You are going to school, hopefully preparing yourself for the career that will provide you with income.

22-65 inches:These are the **accumulation** years. This is the phase of your financial life when you are working, saving and growing your wealth. As you can see, this is the longest phase of your financial life, since it extends from the time we join the workforce up until we retire. Unless you win the lottery or strike it rich with some other windfall, this is the time of your life where your wealth should accumulate steadily over your working years. Take for example an individual whose employer offers a 401(k) program. Small contributions are made each pay period into the retirement savings program. Hopefully, these contributions are matched by your employer. By law, these contributions are tax-deferred and, while there are provisions for taking the money out in case of emergencies or other dire need, they remain in the account and are typically invested in mutual funds administered by a custodian. There is, in fact, a penalty for withdrawing money from the account prior to age 59 ½. If left alone to grow, the account should yield multiple thousands to you when you reach retirement age.

If you make regular contributions to your 401(k) account, you are the beneficiary of a principle of investing called *dollar cost averaging.* The stock market can be volatile, but for a young person willing to invest steadily and consistently over a period of years, the volatility of the stock market can work to their advantage. Let's say you contribute $100 per month into your 401(k) and that money goes to buy shares of a mutual fund. The number of shares purchased each time will not be the same. Since the dollar contribution is static, your contribution will buy more shares when the market is down. That's a good thing. Time is on your side, remember. Those shares will eventually fatten up when the market rebounds. When the market is up, your contribution will buy fewer shares, but that's okay because your account is prospering. You can do no wrong, even in a volatile market, if (a) you have time on your side, and (b) you are patient and consistent with your contributions.

65+ inches: This is the preservation and distribution phase of your financial life. This second phase of retirement investing relates to keeping your retirement savings intact. During the accumulation phase you were trying to grow your nest egg to a certain dollar amount. Now the goal is to keep what you have gained. You may be working, in which case you are still saving. But it won't be long until you pull the plug on the infusion of cash into your account and begin withdrawals to pay bills and support yourself in retirement.

You back off from excessive risk during this phase. You are more interested in the return *of* your money than the return *on* your money. This is what you might call the "red zone" of retirement. In football terms, it is when you are within the 20-yard line. The field is compressed. Every play is critical. Lose the ball here and the opportunity to score is lost and the other team takes over. Your goal in this phase is to maintain your savings pace, reduce market risk and look for somewhere safe to invest your life's savings for your golden years. You want to make sure that your nest egg lasts as long as you do.

Ironically, during the distribution phase, the investing principle that worked in your favor, dollar cost averaging, can work in the reverse. Why? Because now you are taking money out on the same systematic basis you used to create the account in the first place and the fluctuations of the market can be a hindrance instead of a help. Let's say you are 65 and retiring. Because you won't be receiving that steady paycheck any longer, you need income from your 401(k) or IRA to make up the shortfall between your other sources of income and your living expenses. Let's say you have $300,000 in your retirement account. You start withdrawing four percent per year, or $12,000, from your retirement account which is still invested in mutual funds. What happens if the market is down and share prices fall? You are now selling shares each time you make a withdrawal. You must withdraw the same amount each month to cover expenses. If your market-based account drops in value by 20 percent in year one due to a market correction, and you take out your four percent withdrawal, at the end of the first year your $300,000 is down to $230,000.

Taking withdrawals out in years when your account is down in value accelerates the decline. Your old pal, dollar cost averaging, has now turned on you and become *reverse* dollar cost averaging. The solution, of course, is not to take retirement income that you must depend on for living expenses from investments that fluctuate due to market risk.

Earlier in this book we wrote about the pleasant phenomenon that baby boomers are experiencing of living longer. The prevailing concern, however, is outliving one's resources and becoming a burden on loved ones or a ward of the state in old age. How long will you live? That answer is X, the unknown, isn't it? According to data compiled by the Social Security Administration:

- A man reaching age 65 today can expect to live, on average, until age 84.
- A woman turning age 65 today can expect to live, on average, until age 86.

And those are just averages. About one out of every four 65-year-olds today will live past age 90, and one out of 10 will live past age 95.[4]

---

[4] Social Security. "Life Expectancy." https://www.ssa.gov/planners/lifeexpectancy.html

By the way, in doing research for this book we discovered that we could slowly extend the yellow ¾ inch-wide measuring tape horizontally to 85 inches before it buckled. If the inch markings represent the years of our lives, that is an interesting coincidence, don't you think? If you continue to invest in your sixties and seventies the same way you did when you were in your thirties and forties, you may be headed for a nasty spill. Just ask the millions of seniors who were unaware their fortunes were at risk in 2008 and lost billions of dollars because they didn't know where they were, financially speaking.

Surviving the Market Crash

The days surrounding the market crash of 2008 were interesting times for Heise Advisory Group. Our philosophy of investing gives prime importance to managing volatility, so we didn't do too much to change our investing processes during those stormy days on Wall Street. We did, however, meet with many people who were looking for a rescue, who needed help to preserve what was left of their fortunes. Sad to say, some had lost as much as half of their net worth. We felt like first responders at a crash site. People were hurting. We did what we could.

During that time, we felt somewhat justified by our practice of avoiding unnecessary market risks. After all, since we primarily work with people who are in or planning for retirement, we know they won't have as much time to make up market losses. For those who were heavily invested in risk-based assets, 2008 wrecked or at least dented their retirement dreams.

Knowing where you are on the wealth timeline changes your perspective. When you are new to investing, you are rightfully concerned about the return on your investments. After all, you are in the accumulation phase of life. When people choose brokers as their financial advisors, their conversations are usually centered around rates of return and investment gains. Things change, however, when you are past the accumulation phase. At that point, you have amassed a degree of wealth which, when you stop working, must see you through retirement. You now need a true wealth manager. You can't afford to lose a significant portion of a non-renewable resource you depend on for your livelihood.

Please don't misunderstand this part of our message. Your money still needs to work for you at this stage of your financial life. But the order of things is different. Instead of grow, preserve and distribute, the priorities become preserve, distribute and grow. This is why our typical financial plan for retirees calls for growth *only* after their lifetime income has been put in place and the cash flow they need has been established. At *that* point we heartily recommend a portion of the portfolio be placed to optimize growth and offset inflation.

The Heise family with Hall of Famer Whitey Herzog.

CHAPTER 3

Taking Charge of Your Financial Life

"Financial freedom is available to those who learn about it and work for it." ~ Robert Kiyosaki

Whose fault was it that the Titanic sank?

The mood was festive both on the docks in Southampton on the southern coast of England and aboard the massive passenger ship when she departed on her maiden voyage to New York City on April 10, 1912. She was a modern marvel of construction for the time. The Titanic was not only the largest and most luxurious passenger ship ever built, she was the largest man-made moving object to date ever constructed.

Because the Titanic boasted of eight water-tight compartments that would automatically close if the hull was breached, the ship was thought to be unsinkable. Icebergs had been spotted in the North Atlantic along the ship's intended route, but neither the captain, Edward J. Smith, nor any of his crew seemed concerned. This detail was not even brought to the attention of any of the

2,224 passengers aboard, some of whom were the wealthiest people in the world at that time.

So when the ship struck an iceberg four days into the crossing near Newfoundland and sank less than three hours later, whose fault was it? The engineers could have been blamed. When the ship was found on the ocean floor in 1985, it was determined that the glancing collision with the iceberg was too much for the ship's watertight compartments to save her. Was her design, as advanced as it was for the times, still flawed?

Was it the fault of the builders? Recent tests of the steel from the Titanic reveal that the metal was much more brittle than modern steel. A more "impact resistant" steel could have been used but wasn't.

Was it the fault of the marketing people? The idea of a marketing strategy causing a ship to sink might seem a bit strange. But White Star Line marketing people distributed newspaper articles with extravagant claims of an "unsinkable ship," which probably caused much overconfidence. As a result, few if any questioned the shortage of lifeboats (only 20 with a capacity of 65 people each) or the ship's excessive speed.

Captain Smith told the press before leaving the docks at Southampton, "I cannot imagine any condition which would cause this ship to founder. I cannot conceive of any vital disaster happening to this vessel. Modern shipbuilding has gone beyond that."

Was it the captain's fault? In a word, yes. Where was Captain Smith when the ship struck the submerged iceberg? He wasn't on the bridge. He had left the actual piloting of the ship to his first officer, Will Murdoch. It is not clear whether he was enjoying drinks in the ship's lounge or had retired to his room. In any case, he wasn't at the wheel. But he was responsible for guiding the ship safely across the ocean. It didn't matter what the engineers did or didn't do. It didn't matter what the marketing people said or didn't say. It didn't even matter that there were only half as many lifeboats as there should have been. He had ultimate say in all the details.

Are we the captain of our financial ship? Do we know where it is going? Are we in control? We should be. There are some things we can't control, no more than Captain Smith could have controlled icebergs in the North Atlantic in 1912. We can't control the volatility of the stock market, for instance. We can't control interest rates, the national debt or the policy of the Federal Reserve. But there are some things we can control. Of those controllable factors, one of the most important is where you turn for information, or whom you trust.

Where You Turn for Financial Advice

We seem to live in an age of information these days. In fact, we suffer from information overload. Go to any large mega-bookstore and just stand in the middle and look around. Remember when you would actually visit a public library to research something you wanted to know? Imagine how antiquated that process must sound to children of the information age with a smart phone in their hand capable of accessing the internet and finding details on virtually any topic imaginable with a few taps of their fingers. Alvin Toffler, author of Future Shock, predicted way back in 1970 that the rapidly increasing amounts of information being produced in coming decades would be problematic for society. He said we would become jaded, overwhelmed and mistrustful in the face of too many words coming at us with increasing velocity from a variety of sources. He popularized the expression, "information overload."

We are beset by an investment advice tsunami. Stroll through the magazine section of a large book store and check out how many total magazines there are on anything and everything. Then look at how many financial magazines there are on the racks. It will blow your mind. Look at the headlines. If you were to buy all of them and read all of them, do you think you would know any more about how to captain your financial ship than you did when you walked into the store?

"Buy Gold!"

"Don't Buy Gold!"

"Buy Petroleum Now!"

"Dump Petroleum Now!"

Remember the days of television with rabbit ears and only 12 channels on the dial? You may be a baby boomer if you can remember the days before cable TV. These days you can get hundreds of channels and dozens of financial news channels at the flick of a remote button. Have you ever seen financial analysts arguing on screen like children on a playground? This may be good for ratings, but it doesn't educate and inform and it certainly does not help us guide our financial ship through treacherous waters.

One financial expert comes onto the set with his coat off and his sleeves rolled up. He gives stock picking advice to the sound of cowbells and slide whistles and talks loudly, like he has had too much coffee. It would be comedic if it weren't for the fact that people actually heed his advice, sometimes to their financial detriment. One of his most famous gaffes happened just prior to the 2008 market meltdown, when he vociferously proclaimed that Bear Stearns, the soon-to-fail mega bank, was in no trouble and a good place to keep your money.

The truth is, no one knows the future and no one can tell which way the stock market is going to go. That is one of the reasons why it makes such excellent grist for the media. People love a prognosticator. It entertains us. When we are in front of a class or an audience we will sometimes ask for a show of hands:

How many think the stock market will go up this year? A few hands go up.

How many think the stock market will go down this year? A few hands go up.

How many haven't got a clue? Nearly all the hands go up.

They are telling the truth. If we knew that we would all be on a beach somewhere with not a care in the world hiring someone to count our money.

Where Do You Turn for Financial Advice?

If you want to invest, to whom do you turn or from what source do you seek financial advice? When we ask that question to a group, here's a typical list:

- Broker
- Financial Advisor (Fiduciary)
- Insurance Agent
- Wealthy people
- Friends
- Relatives
- The internet
- Magazines
- Newspapers
- Financial channels on TV
- Radio
- Attorney

Not mentioned, but should have been:
- Next door neighbor
- The guy at the office who is always hanging out in the coffee room.

What happens when their advice doesn't pan out? What is their response?

"The market goes up and the market goes down."

"Just hang in there and it will all be okay."

The only problem with hanging in there is it requires time. If you are in your accumulation phase of life, time is on your side. But if you are approaching or in retirement do you have that kind of time? How long do you have to hang in there? Six months? Six years? 10 years?

It used to be that such decisions were not as critical. We had pensions. Work for a company for 20 years, get a gold watch and a nice pension. The prevailing thinking was, "Who cares about the stock market? I got a pension for the rest of my life and all is good." But these days it is our responsibility to carve out our own financial security.

Personal versus Product Advice

All of us, at one time or another, have been sold a product and later scratched our head and said to ourselves, "Why in the world did I buy that?" Product salespeople exist in the financial world too. Based on our observations, the majority of financial services are built around the sale of a financial product. The individuals who sell these products can call themselves a "financial advisor" and even put that on their office door, their business cards and the name plate on their desk, but that doesn't make them a true financial advisor. Their job is to sell a product.

When Abraham Lincoln found himself in a situation where he was trying to make others see the truth over a misrepresentation of the facts, he is reported to have asked, "How many legs does a dog have if you call the tail a leg?" He would wait for the response to come back from the other party, no doubt proud of his math skills, "Five."

"No," Abe would say in that slow, deliberate way he had of speaking. "The answer is four. Just calling the tail a leg doesn't make it one."

Calling oneself a financial advisor does not necessarily make one a financial advisor. Agents and brokers will sometimes use the financial advisor label when they are really just product salesman. They make a profit, either for themselves or for their company. Their advice is built around the distribution of a financial product and enhancing their enterprise.

In the American free enterprise system, there is nothing wrong with making a profit or earning a commission. It is done every day and there is nothing illegal or unethical about it. But the rub comes in when individuals set themselves up in the public eye as one who is offering unbiased independent advice when such is not really the case.

In fact, this issue has come to the attention of some of the highest financial officials in the country. A few years ago, the Department of Labor wrote a new regulation, somewhat anticlimactically called the "DOL Fiduciary Rule." To understand what this rule is getting at, you must first understand the word "fiduciary," which means someone who is legally obligated to act on behalf of someone else and represent their personal best interests. In a financial capacity, this means a financial advisor who is a fiduciary can only recommend the products that are the best fit for a client's unique situation instead of recommending a product based on the commission or pay the advisor would get in return.

The DOL Fiduciary Rule was meant to apply to all financial recommendations surrounding someone's retirement assets. Of course, many in the financial services industry pushed back, repeatedly asking for delays and exemptions, so the rule was delayed multiple times and finally vacated just before the completion of this book, destined to fade into history. But at Heise Advisory Group, we pride ourselves as already being fiduciaries and acting in the best interests of our clients, regardless of federal regulations and mandates.

In St. Louis, Missouri, where we live and work, headlines of kickbacks from mutual fund companies to a well-known brokerage house dominated the financial page after a brokerage house reportedly paid a $75 million penalty for not disclosing the revenue-sharing agreement it had with fund companies. That is a perfect example of selling products instead of offering unbiased financial advice. Did the people who came to them for financial advice because they billed themselves as financial advisors know their recommendations were tainted by profit motive? Likely not.

Shouldn't your financial plan be built around you? Shouldn't it be transparent when it comes to fees and charges? Shouldn't it be focused on your goals, your dreams, your plans for the future, your budget, your expenses, preserving your wealth for your retirement and your legacy to your heirs? Of course!

Fiduciary versus Suitability Advice

In the investment field, those who issue advice professionally are obligated to adhere to one of two standards — fiduciary or suitability. The difference between the two is significant. Investment Advisor Representatives who work through Registered Investment Advisors, for example, are bound to a fiduciary standard that was established as part of the Investment Advisors Act of 1940. They are regulated by the SEC or state securities regulators and are required legally to put their client's interests above their own.

The term "fiduciary" comes from the Latin word "fiducia," which means "to trust." We get our English words "confidentiality" and "fidelity" from the same Latin root word. Keep in mind, this is not a decision that an advisor makes on a case by case basis, nor is it a request that the client makes. As we outlined earlier, a fiduciary is legally bound and contractually obligated to give his or her client advice that is in the client's best interest and not motivated by profit or commission. Fiduciaries are not allowed to be self-serving in their counsel. Does that mean that they do not receive payment for their services? Not at all! But it is against the law for them to let that remuneration for their expertise and counsel influence or interfere with their advice on a matter pertaining to your financial affairs. In other words, they are not salespersons. They are professional counselors whose obligation is to you and you alone. They are required tell you what is best for you even if they do not benefit one bit. A fiduciary should only provide investment advice based on accurate and complete information. Any analysis given by a fiduciary is required to be thorough, showing both sides. A fiduciary avoids conflicts of interest and is required to disclose even a possible conflict of interest.

So, what is a suitability standard and what's wrong with that? Nothing is wrong with suitability. In fact, any advice given to you by a fiduciary must be suitable for you to be in your best interest. Suitability means that the agent or broker who sells you an insurance or investment product has to reasonably believe that the product or investment is fitting for you based on your circumstances. Brokers, for example, are regulated by the Financial Industry Regulatory Authority (FINRA). Brokers are not legally obligated to place his or her interests below that of the client.

A key distinction in terms of loyalty also exists. A broker's duty is to the broker-dealer he or she works for, not necessarily the client served. Other descriptions of suitability include making sure transaction costs are not excessive or that a recommendation is not unsuitable for a client. It would be unsuitable, for example, for an insurance agent to sell a policy to someone who could not afford the premiums. On the investment side of things, examples that may violate suitability include excessive trading, churning the account simply to generate more commissions or frequently switching account assets to generate transaction income for the broker-dealer. Also, the need to disclose potential conflicts of interest is not as strict a requirement for brokers; an investment must only be suitable. It doesn't necessarily have to be consistent with the individual investor's objectives and profile.

Please understand that this does not mean that we believe that brokers are unethical or plan to harm their clients. To the contrary, we feel confident that most brokers are ethical and do not intend harm to their clients.

Doing the Right Thing

It's okay to ask how your financial advisor gets paid. Most of us were brought up to think it rude and inappropriate to ask such a bold question. I agree that it may be an impertinent question for polite conversation, but this is different. We are entrusting someone with what is perhaps our life's savings. Wouldn't it be a good idea to find out if there is a possible conflict of interest?

We have individuals come to our office from time to time and let us know that they have been with a certain financial advisor for several years. They say they trust and like the person. When I ask them if they know how their advisor gets paid, most say no. But considering the foregoing information about fiduciary versus suitability standards, don't you think it is a legitimate question? Consider this: If your advisor only receives a commission when he or she sells you something or makes changes to your mutual funds, could that possibly influence their recommendations? Could a profit motive possibly enter into the decision? If the advisor says he or she is paid by a fee, isn't it in your best interests to know how much the fee is, who pays the fee, what comprises the fee and how often they charge the fee?

We aren't saying that commissions and fees are wrong. Have you ever booked a flight or planned a vacation through a travel agency? They can provide you with excellent service and sometimes save you a small fortune and you never pay them a penny. They shop for the best accommodations for you and attempt to save you money on fares, knowing they will receive compensation from the provider. There's nothing wrong with that. It would be wrong if you flew on a non-competitive airline and stayed at a substandard hotel because the travel agent was more interested in making money than seeing to it that your travel needs were met. Likewise, if your advisor, or the candidate you are interviewing for that professional service, doesn't seem forthcoming or willing to answer your questions quickly and clearly, it could be an indication that perhaps you should look elsewhere.

Is the Advice Independent?

What's wrong with the following picture? You are shopping for a car and you want to receive the most unbiased advice possible on which make and model to buy. So, you go to your local Ford dealership and ask the staff there for their opinions. What are the odds of receiving unbiased advice? Slim to none! The same thing applies to financial advice. As a rule of thumb, it is never in your best interest to take advice from an advisor who works for one company, is loyal to that one company and whose solutions are limited to what that one company can provide. To quote the famous psychologist Abraham Maslow, "If you only have a hammer, you tend to see every problem as a nail."

The financial advice on which you rely needs to be independent to eliminate the possibility of slant and bias. A compass cannot operate properly if a magnet lies close by. The magnetic pull will swing the needle toward the invisible force and create a false reading. It's the same way with financial advice. If the opinions of your advisor are pulled in the direction of a parent company that holds the agent or broker captive to its products or services, it won't serve you well. A fiduciary, on the other hand, is "free to move about the country" as Southwest Airlines commercials say. They are free to use whatever company they need to to provide the best financial services to their clients.

An Important Disclosure

Don't disclosures on medicine advertisements just kill you? Well, not really. In fact, they could save your life. It is a bit amusing how they proclaim all the virtues of some miracle cure, only to follow up with the information that taking the drug could cause vomiting, diarrhea or death! Doesn't necessarily make you feel all that confident about asking your doctor about it, does it? But the drug manufacturer is required to put that information in there; the Food and Drug Administration makes them. Just as the FDA regulates pharmaceutical companies as to our health, the SEC regulates the financial profession, requiring full disclosure on matters pertaining to our wealth.

Reading disclosures can seem like deciphering a bunch of mumbo jumbo but they contain critical information. The reason why disclosures are in fine print sometimes is because those who produce them don't necessarily want you to notice them. But often they contain information you need to make an informed decision. Take this disclosure, for example. Notice the wording the SEC requires broker-dealers to include in their client agreements:

"Your account is a brokerage account and not an advisory account. Our interests may not always be the same as yours. Please ask us questions to make sure you understand your rights and our obligations to you, including the extent of our obligations to disclose conflicts of interest and to act in your best interest. We are paid both by you and, sometimes, by people who compensate us based on what you buy. Therefore, our profits, and our salespersons' compensation, may vary by product and over time."

Were you looking for an advisor? Were you led to believe that the person with whom you were talking operated in that capacity? A 65-year-old woman came to our office recently seeking financial advice. She had just taken a buy-out on her pension program, and now found herself responsible for $1.2 million. She had no expertise or knowledge when it came to managing money or making financial decisions. She had less than $1,000 in her checking account. In this instance, the woman had consulted a broker who honestly told her that he was not a financial advisor and that she needed to consult one. We were appreciative that the broker had taken the time to explain the difference and had been upfront and honest with her. Not all financial professionals have that quality of character.

Taking Ownership of Your Finances

Shortly after the 2008 market meltdown a couple came to our office and were noticeably upset. As they told us their story we could see why. They were both 63 years old and jointly owned and operated a nursery. The business had started small in the early 1980s and had grown to encompass several acres. One of the reasons why they were so successful was because it was obvious that they loved plants and took it personally if a customer was dissatisfied. For 30 years they had gone out of their way to make sure their customers — landscapers, homeowners and builders — were happy.

As is often the case, they were much too wrapped up in making a success out of their business to look after the money it generated. They had plowed most of their earnings back into the business which was debt free. The rest of their money they placed in the hands of what they thought was a financial advisory firm, confident that they were in good hands. They were on a first-name basis with the people who managed their money and never questioned their advice. They opened the statements from their broker and filed them away. As long as the numbers were up they believed all was well.

The couple's plans were to retire at age 65, sign over the nursery to their children, who were fully capable of operating it, and take to the Retirement Highway in a motor home they had plans of purchasing. They had taken few vacations in the last 25 years and planned to make up for that in retirement. The woman had a special briefcase in which she kept maps and travel guides with the corners of the pages turned down on places they wished to visit.

Then the market crash of 2008 occurred and they lost nearly half of their nest egg. The broker was apologetic but said there was nothing he could do. He told them to hang in there.

In the end, there was no way around the fact that they would have to work at least two years past their retirement goal. The blue highways on the map would have to wait until they could rebuild their savings and convert some of their paid-for property into cash.

"We should have paid more attention," the wife said.

She was right. It is important to trust those managing your money but not blindly. Know where your assets are and know why they are there. Ask questions until you understand your investment strategies. Take the time to read the fine print. All fine print may not be evil, but there is truth in that old axiom, "The devil is in the details." You are ultimately captain of your financial ship. Don't abrogate your duties!

Lori and Ken Heise, 2005, cheering on the Green Bay Packers in Lambeau Stadium.

CHAPTER 4

Finding "Your Number" for Retirement

"If you want to rear financial blessings, you have to sow financially."
~ Joel Osteen

One question we hear a lot in the financial planning profession is: "How much money do I need to retire?" It's a bit of a loaded question because there is no easy answer. What is the right number for one person may not be the right number for another. That's one reason for consulting a retirement income specialist. They are supposed to be able to help you arrive at a concrete number so you can plan your life. So, the shortest answer to the "how much" question is, "It depends."

One of the cleverest television commercials we have seen on the "how much" question involved a man walking his dog down a neighborhood sidewalk. Under his free arm he is carrying what looks like an enormous number. You can't make out exactly what the number is but you can see that it says one million dollars and change. That's what gets your attention, of course — the incongruity of a man strolling down a tree-lined street with a huge number under his arm.

Then we see another man standing on a ladder trimming a hedge. Beside him on the top of the hedge is the word "Gazillion." Hedge-trimmer asks dog-walker, "Hey, Clark, whatcha got there?" and points with his shears to the number under his arm.

"It's my number," says the dog walker. "It's the amount I need to save to retire the way I want."

That's the whole point of the commercial. The man walking his dog is the smart one. He has figured out to the penny what he needs to retire while his hedge trimming neighbor doesn't have a clue. He just guessed at it and came up with the nebulous "Gazillion".

"Is that your number...Gazillion?" the dog walker asks with a wry smile.

Hedge trimmer shrugs and says, "Yeah. Gazillion, bazillion...it's just a guess."

"How do you plan for *that?*" asks the dog walker, furrowing his brow, to which hedge trimmer confesses, "I just blindly throw money at it and hope something good happens." The commercial ends with the embarrassed hedge trimmer blowing a lock of hair out of his eyes and issuing a nervous laugh as if to say, "I know I'm stupid."

Other than it being a pitch to allow the producers of the commercial to help you plan for retirement, we couldn't figure out what they are advertising. But the point was clearly made that to have an effective plan for retirement, you first need to ascertain what your individual number (or nest egg, as some call it) needs to be. You also won't get there by just throwing money at it and hoping something good will happen. Hope is a good thing, but it is not a plan.

The best way to get to your number is to back into it. First, we work together to determine approximately what your budget will look like in retirement. Once we nail that down we can figure out how much you will need in place before you turn in your notice and unplug yourself from your job. In the commercial, the man with the specific number had obviously taken the time to sit down with a professional planner and work out these general details, which is why he had a specific number and the other man, the one with Gazillion, only had a hazy guess. The moral of the story is that if you fail to plan, you are, by default, planning to fail.

What else is accomplished by knowing your number? You know where you stand financially. It could be that you need to work longer than you had expected or get a second job. That may not be the sweetest news in the world, but it is essential knowledge in planning for the future. It may also be that you need to pare down your lifestyle and save more. Perhaps you will need to make some other adjustment. But for those with no plan, it doesn't really matter, does it? You're just like the hedge trimmer with his Gazillion. To quote Lewis Carroll, "If you don't know where you're going any road will take you there."

Why The Four Percent Rule Doesn't Work Anymore

Most people want to make sure they can live as comfortably in retirement as they did before. It used to be that the "Four Percent Sustainable Withdrawal Rule" was regarded as the "holy grail" of retirement analysis. What is the Four Percent Rule? It is a concept largely endorsed around the finance community by stock brokers. They said if you have a brokerage account you can withdraw four percent from it every year, and as long as you rebalance the account each year with the appropriate mix of stocks and bonds, you won't run out of money… for 30 years! To make the math simple, if you have $1 million in the account, you could ostensibly withdraw $40,000 per year for 30 years. The reason why we refer to the four percent rule in the past tense here is because it doesn't work anymore.

The concept was developed in the mid-1990s by three professors at Trinity University in San Antonio, Texas. As an economic science project, the professors were attempting to arrive at the "magic percent" of withdrawal for retirement. They tinkered with various percentages until they came up with four. There were lots of assumptions, however. First, for their projections to work, the market had to continue performing according to their expectations, which were based on a 70-year look back. Because they took their data from a stock market that was performing at its zenith, all looked rosy. Why wouldn't it? In 1995 the stock market knew only one direction — North! If you look back from that pinnacle, the only hiccup the market had since the Great Depression of the 1930s was a dramatic but brief drop in 1987.

Wall Street applauded the four percent rule when the three professors released their findings in 1998. Stock brokers pounced on it as if it were the best thing since sliced bread and vanilla ice cream. Many brokers still preach it as if it were gospel, but the math doesn't work if you input the latest market data. Two severe market crashes occurred in the decade of 2000; In fact, market analysts dubbed the 2000s as the "lost decade" because the market was extremely volatile but in the end neither gained nor lost. You can't really blame the professors. They had no way of knowing. But to drag out the four percent rule these days as a working formula for retirement is whipping a dead horse.

One of the best research papers on the four percent rule was co-authored by William Sharpe, the winner of the 1990 Nobel Prize in economics. The title of his report, released in April 2008, was *The 4%Rule — At What Price?* and it labels the four percent retirement rule as outdated and unworkable.[5] You don't have to be a genius to come to that conclusion, however. To draw $40,000 per year you would have to start with a million dollars. Few people have that much money saved for retirement. There are no guarantees as to which way the market will go and therefore no guarantees as to how long the money will last.

Most financial advisors waved goodbye to the Four Percent Withdrawal Rule after the market crash of 2008, acknowledging that the formula on which it was based simply didn't work. How did it ever become a "rule" in the first place?

In the early 1990s, William P. Bengen, a California financial planner, had been crunching numbers and running projections to determine what percentage a retired person could safely withdraw from his or her brokerage account per year for 30 years and not run out of money. He worked with different rates of withdrawal, as well as different allocations of assets to come up with just the right number. It is important here to understand that two things were assumed: (a) All the assets would be invested in the stock market, and (b) the duration of the retirement would be 30 years.

Bengen's research appeared in the *Journal of Financial Planning* under an article he wrote entitled, "Determining Withdrawal Rates Using Historical Data."[6] The magic number turned out to be 4.5 percent. Bengen tinkered with many scenarios, using 30-year spans of market data beginning with 1926 and working forward. With that historical data in place on the left side, he then tinkered with the withdrawal rate on the right side, always including in his historical data the effects of inflation. Bengen's idea was that if the portfolio was properly balanced — 60 percent stocks and 40

[5] Jason S. Scott, William F. Sharpe, and John G. Watson. April 2008. "The 4% Rule – At What Price?" https://web.stanford.edu/~wfsharpe/retecon/4percent.pdf.

[6] William P. Bengen. Journal of Financial Planning. October 1994. "Determining Withdrawal Rates Using Historical Data."
http://www.retailinvestor.org/pdf/Bengen1.pdf.

percent bonds — and tweaked periodically, it could withstand the effects of the consistent withdrawals and a 4.15 percent rate of inflation and last for three decades.

Financial advisors in the brokerage community were ecstatic. They latched onto Bengen's formula. There was nothing wrong with Bengen's research. It was all well-documented, and the math seemed to work. Bengen was a graduate of the Massachusetts Institute of Technology who managed a soft-drink bottling company before becoming a financial planner, but he was obviously one of the better minds in the business to have even come up with such a plan.

So what went wrong? Why have so many in the financial advisory community distanced themselves from Bengen's formula as if it were curdled milk or a communicable disease? Why have highly-regarded financial publications in the last few years published articles proclaiming the Four Percent Withdrawal Rule is officially dead? Bengen did thorough research, and his figures included the Great Depression era when it came to stock market returns. His inflation numbers also took into account the hyper-inflation years of the late 1970s when Jimmy Carter was president. The problem was, Bengen based his conclusions on data available to him at the time, when the market was on a roll and had not experienced the dot-com bubble burst of 2000 and the Financial Crisis of 2008 with its accompanying Great Recession and the sideways market of 2000-2010.

An article entitled, "Say Goodbye to the 4% Rule," written by Kelly Greene, appeared in the March 1, 2013 issue of the Wall Street Journal.[7] The article included this damning paragraph which shows just how flawed Bengen's formula when projected over the most recent data:

---

[7] Kelly Greene. The Wall Street Journal. March 3, 2013. "Say Goodbye to the 4% Rule." https://www.wsj.com/articles/say-goodbye-to-the-4-rule-1376315815.

"If you had retired Jan. 1, 2000, with an initial 4 percent withdrawal rate and a portfolio of 55 percent stocks and 45 percent bonds rebalanced each month, with the first year's withdrawal amount increased by 3 percent a year for inflation, your portfolio would have fallen by a third through 2010, according to investment firm T. Rowe Price Group. And you would be left with only a 29 percent chance of making it through three decades, the firm estimates."

The Heise family strikes a pose in Busch Stadium at a client event in 2013.

CHAPTER 5

The Other Side
of Retirement Mountain

"Retirement is like a long vacation in Las Vegas. The goal is to enjoy it the fullest, but not so fully that you run out of money." ~ Jonathan Clements

British mountaineer George Mallory wanted to be the first person to climb Mount Everest, the world's tallest peak. In 1924, when a New York Times reporter asked him why, he gave the famous witty response, "Because it's there!"

Did he ever make it to the top? We will never know. In the spring of 1999, American climber Eric Simonson found Mallory's frozen corpse on the mountain's north face and identified the body as that of the British climber by tags attached to the lining of his clothing. The body was intact, preserved in shallow ice since 1924. The broken bones, dislocated shoulder and the ropes wrapped around his torso suggested that he had fallen or died in an avalanche. He had tried to scale Everest twice before and failed. The great unanswered question was whether or not Mallory and his climbing partner, Andrew Irvine, had made it to the summit.

Did they die on their way up, or on their way down? Mountain climbing archivists are still debating that question.

According to some estimates, 80 percent of climbing accidents occur on the trip down the mountain. Let's face it: The ultimate goal of climbing a mountain is not merely to reach the peak, it's to descend safely and live to tell about it.

Why is making it down the other side of the mountain so dangerous? Largely because all the preparation and planning focuses on the climb. The risks of the descent get far less consideration. On Mount Everest, most deaths occur in the "Death Zone," just above 26,000 feet *on the way down.*

It's the same way with successful retirement planning. Most people and most financial advisors tend to focus on getting *to* retirement. Brokers and mutual fund managers deal almost exclusively with rates of return and the accumulation side of wealth management. Far too little attention is given to getting us *through* retirement. True, we can't have one without the other. We must invest, save and accumulate to get up the mountain, but carefully managing and preserving those assets so we can distribute them during retirement is the ultimate goal.

The pre-retirement question most often asked is, "Do I have enough?" But the real question is, "How much can I safely withdraw without running out?" This is especially true since there are so many real and present dangers that can affect us during this life phase.

Cash for emergencies, for example. Does your retirement plan include a liquid emergency fund? What if you are retired, living on a fixed income with very little margin, and the roof needs replacing, the car dies, or a loved one suddenly needs your financial support? Having an emergency fund can help keep you from dipping into your reserves — reserves that you must keep working for you if you are to continue your current standard of living throughout retirement.

We are living longer. Will your longevity outlive your assets? Have you and your financial advisor positioned your assets in such a way as to prevent that from happening?

The stock market can be volatile. Can your retirement income withstand the sequence of returns trap to which so many retirement portfolios are exposed? How about inflation? Will that erosive force eat away at the returns on your investments? If 70 percent of all people over the age of 65 will end up needing some kind of long-term care, will you be one of them or will you dodge that bullet? How about the legacy you leave behind for loved ones? Will it be a legacy of debt or wealth?

Retirement should be a pleasant period, not one fraught with worry and fear. Planning makes that possible, yet from what we read and observe relatively few Americans see the urgency of it. Whenever we sit down with folks to discuss making it down the "backside of the mountain," so to speak, we always start with cash flow management and how to direct your resources. We use wealth-accumulation strategies to determine where you are now and what is the most efficient route for reaching your ultimate objective. Everyone is different in this respect. Some couples want to spend every last dime of their resources and leave nothing when they go. We saw a bumper sticker on the back of a motor home that read, "We are spending our children's inheritance." As it turns out, we made friends with the couple who owned it and found out they were quite serious about it! Their two children were both well-educated professionals, successful in their own right, and needed no financial help from their parents.

Others we know, however, want to live as frugally as possible so they can leave as much of their wealth as possible to their children and grandchildren. When we build and design a *Retirement Roadmap Review®* for clients, we put safeguards in place to protect income against the most common dangers that present themselves on the "other side of the mountain" five or ten years into retirement. We review the plan and update our strategies periodically—at least annually. Why? Because times change and people change with the times. What was relevant when you began retirement may not be relevant five years into it. What fit your goals *then* may not fit them *now*.

You Need a Sherpa

Sherpa is Tibetan for "eastern people." In the high country of Nepal, deep in the Himalayan Mountains, members of this ethnic group are highly respected for their skills. They know the mountains so well that their name has become a synonym for "mountain guide". No mountain climber in his right mind would think of attempting to climb Mount Everest without first hiring a Sherpa. On April 18, 2014, newspapers around the world ran the headline that 16 Sherpas were killed in an avalanche on Mount Everest. It was the single deadliest climbing accident in the mountain's history. Ironically, the route on which the Sherpas were killed was one of the easiest routes up the mountain — the same one used by Sir Edmund Hillary and his Sherpa, Tenzing Norgay, in 1953.

Just as choosing the route to ascend and descend a mountain is a critical decision, choosing the best way up and down Retirement Mountain is a big decision. Doing so alone without the help of a skilled and competent financial advisor could spell disaster. Some climbers die on the descent because they fail to take time to acclimatize to the high altitude. Sherpas, on the other hand, live their entire lives at high altitudes. The euphoria of having "made it to the top" creates in some climbers an overconfidence that causes them to take needless risk on the way down. Is there a parallel here to retirement planning? New retirees sometimes tend to invest the same way in their retirement years as they did when they were in their working years. The fact is, strategies that got you *to* retirement may not get you **through** retirement. Take dollar-cost averaging for example. We talked about that in chapter two of this book, "Knowing Where You Are Financially." Dollar-cost averaging was great during your working years, but reverse dollar-cost averaging can bite you in the backside in retirement if you do not plan properly.

The "Sequence of Returns" Trap

Another financial phenomenon that can spell disaster on the backside of Retirement Mountain is the "sequence of returns trap." Here are two truths regarding investing when you are in retirement:

- Market losses affect us more severely the older we become because we have less time in a volatile market to wait for our portfolio to recover.
- The severity of these losses is exacerbated by the fact that we are withdrawing money from our accounts.

As the chef told the cook when he burned the steaks, "Timing is everything." During the accumulation phase of our life, did it really matter if we had a crash in the stock market, such as the one that occurred in 1987? If you were in the market during that period, you had time on your side. Despite the near capsize, Wall Street found her keel and the good ship "Free Enterprise" righted herself. Your portfolio experienced a little dry spell, and its leaves withered a bit. But the blooms eventually came back, and new growth appeared.

What if you encounter the same situation when you are on the cusp of retirement? For one thing, time is no longer on your side.

The market may take years — years you do not have — to rebound. Compounding the matter is the fact that you must make withdrawals from your accumulated savings just to pay the bills. You can neither control the stock market nor time it. The only adjustment you can make is how much you invest in the market and where you invest it.

To see how sequence of returns can affect a retiree, consider the example of Harry and Bob. Everything is the same about the accounts of Harry and Bob. They both start out with nest eggs of $500,000 at age 65. They each begin withdrawing five percent from their accounts annually, or $25,000 per year. Anticipating inflation, they each plan to up the amount they withdraw each year by three percent. So, the first year of their retirement, they withdraw $25,000, the next year $25,750, and the next year $26,552.50, and so on.

Just for illustration's sake, let's put both Harry and Bob's portfolio all in a single index fund that mirrors exactly the movement of the market. Whatever the stock market did is what happened in their identical accounts. Let's let them both experience an *average* 8.03 percent gain over 24 years. If you are wondering where we are going with this, we took an actual slice of market history here and tracked it, so that part of it is realistic. What is not realistic, and what makes the point here, is that, although Harry and Bob receive the exact same returns, we reversed the order in which they received those returns. In our scenario, what happened in Harry's account at age 65 happened in Bob's account at age 89. We had to do it this way to show you how important "sequence of returns" really is.

The market will do what the market will do. There were years of gains and years of losses in each account. In each account, however, there was a period when the market went down appreciably three years in a row. The losses were the same. The losses hit Harry early in retirement. The losses hit Bob toward the end.

What a difference timing makes! Because Harry experienced the market losses early in his retirement, he ended up running out of money at age 83. Here he is, draining his account steadily for his living expenses while market losses are bleeding it from the other end. His account is hit harder because it was hit early. There was much less invested to take advantage of the upswing when the market bounced back.

Bob's losses occurred farther down the road. The market lost the same percentage, but the amount of loss was much less in Bob's account because of the sequence. Bob still had plenty of money left to fund his retirement.

This is one reason why when brokers project "average" returns, they are telling the truth. But average returns don't tell the whole story. When you hear, "Statistically, the stock market has returned an average of 8% per year," your mind infers…"and that is the rate at which my nest egg will grow." Maybe not. It depends on the sequence of those returns (or losses) as to whether your experience will be favorable or unfavorable.

Bob's Market Losses:	Harry's Market Losses:
-23.37% at age 87	-10.14% at age 65
-13.04% at age 88	-13.04% at age 66
-10.14% at age 89	-23.37% at age 67

Bob

Age	Hypothetical stock market gains	Withdrawal at start of year	Nest egg at start of year
64			$500,000
65	12.78%	$25,000	$500,000
66	23.45%	$25,750	$535,716
67	26.38%	$26,523	$629,575
68	3.53%	$27,318	$762,140
69	13.62%	$28,138	$760,755
70	3.00%	$28,982	$832,396
71	-38.49%	$29,851	$827,524
72	26.38%	$30,747	$490,684
73	19.53%	$31,669	$581,270
74	26.67%	$32,619	$656,916
75	31.10%	$33,598	$790,788
76	20.26%	$34,606	$991,981
77	34.11%	$35,644	$1,151,375
78	-1.54%	$36,713	$1,496,314
79	7.06%	$37,815	$1,437,133
80	4.46%	$38,949	$1,498,042
81	26.31%	$40,118	$1,524,231
82	-6.56%	$41,321	$1,874,535
83	27.25%	$42,561	$1,712,970
84	12.40%	$43,838	$2,125,604
85	2.03%	$45,153	$2,339,923
86	14.37%	$46,507	$2,341,297
87	-23.27%	$47,903	$2,630,297
88	-13.04%	$49,340	$1,978,993
89	-10.14%	$50,820	$1,677,975
Average Return	8.03%	Total Withdrawal	$911,482

Harry

Age	Hypothetical stock market gains	Withdrawal at start of year	Nest egg at start of year
64			$500,000
65	**-10.14%**	$25,000	$500,000
66	**-13.04%**	$25,750	$426,839
67	**-23.37%**	$26,523	$348,776
68	14.62%	$27,318	$246,956
69	2.03%	$28,138	$251,750
70	12.40%	$28,982	$228,146
71	27.25%	$29,851	$223,862
72	-6.65%	$30,747	$246,879
73	26.31%	$31,669	$201,956
74	4.46%	$32,619	$215,084
75	7.06%	$33,598	$190,610
76	-1.54%	$34,606	$168,090
77	34.11%	$35,644	$131,429
78	20.26%	$36,713	$128,458
79	31.01%	$37,815	$110,335
80	26.67%	$38,949	$95,008
81	19.53%	$40,118	$71,009
82	26.38%	$36,923	$36,923
83	-38.49%	$0	$0
84	3.00%		
85	13.62%		
86	3.53%		
87	26.38%		
88	23.45%		
89	12.78%		
Average Return	**8.03%**	**Total Withdrawal**	**$580,963**

Average versus Actual

Averages can be tricky. If you have one foot in a bucket of ice water and your other foot in a bucket of hot water, one could argue that your feet's AVERAGE temperature is comfortable. When you calculate average returns, losses and gains are equal in weight. Imagine a balance sheet where you have a column on the left for gains and one on the right for losses. In row one, you have a 50 percent gain on the left and a 50 percent loss on the right. That leaves you with an average return of zero. Let's put some real numbers to it. If you invested $100,000, which experienced a 50 percent gain and a 50 percent loss over two years, you would have an average return of zero.

Where it gets interesting is when you calculate your *actual* return over your *average* return. Take your $100,000 and apply a 50 percent gain to it. How much do you have now? $150,000, right? Now, take the $150,000 and apply a 50 percent loss to it. How much do you have now? Your account now contains only $75,000. What does that prove? That losses have a greater weight than gains when you calculate actual dollars.

How would you like to make an investment that earned an *average rate of return* of 25 percent over two years? "That would be fantastic," you reply. Well, let's think about it in terms of *actual returns.* You invest $100,000 and earn 100 percent return in year one. Your money doubles to $200,000. In year two, you lose 50 percent. You are back to $100,000. You averaged a 25 percent rate of return but your real rate of return was zero.

In my opinion, using average returns to illustrate how a portfolio might perform resembles the kind of sleight of hand magicians and illusionists are known for. What you see is not necessarily what you get. Actual returns, on the other hand, are transparent.

Bull, Bear Markets

Somewhere in our family photograph archives is a picture of us in New York City posing beside a big bronze statue of a charging bull. The statue is massive (18 feet long and over 10 feet high) but very lifelike; his eyes are angry and glaring, his nostrils are flared, and if you stand in front of him, you feel as if you are about to be trampled by thundering hooves or impaled by his menacing horns.

"Where's the bear?" we asked the tour guide.

"There is no bear," the tour guide replied.

Since the bull and bear are opposing symbols of the feast and famine cycles of the stock market, we just assumed that the bull's counterpart would be nearby.

We would later learn that a local New York artist, Arturo Di Modica, had started work on the three and a half-ton statue in response to the 1987 stock market crash. He waited until the dead of night on December 15 and deposited the huge statue in front of the New York Stock Exchange as a surprise Christmas gift to the city. He would later say that the Charging Bull

> "The recovery time from the 2007-09 bear market — which coincided with the worst economic downturn since the 1930s — was 5.3 years. In January 2013 the stock market surpassed the level at which it stood on Oct. 9, 2007."
>
> ~ Mark Hulbert, The Wall Street Journal. March 7, 2014. "How to prepare for the next bear market."

represented the vigorous spirit of American enterprise. City officials moved the Charging Bull to Bowling Green Park near the financial district where it has become one of lower Manhattan's favorite tourist attractions. The Charging Bull even has its own web cam at chargingbull.com/video.html.

According to Wall Street lingo, a bull market is when the market is on a positive roll for an extended period, and a bear market is just the opposite. The bull and the bear seem to be apt metaphors. When the market is on a roll, the mood is that of an aggressive feeding frenzy — a stampede, like the bulls tearing through the streets of Pamplona. When the market goes into deep retreat, the snarling bear exits his cave and lurks about, sending investors running for cover, selling off positions and shorting the market.

Technically speaking, a bear market is where the market goes down 20 percent from peak to valley over a period of at least two months, usually measured from a market index, such as the S&P 500. Bear markets are a natural market phenomenon. They are bound to happen. So what's the big deal? The big deal is if we are approaching retirement we could end up caught in a down cycle from which we may not be able to quickly recover if we need to use our invested resources to maintain our lifestyle.

The lesson we can learn from history is not to get nabbed on the downside of the ebb cycle at the wrong time. As we saw earlier, a few years on the wrong square of the financial checkerboard can cost us dearly in retirement.

The Heises and friends cheer on the Cardinals vs. the Angels
at a baseball game in Los Angeles.

CHAPTER 6

Where Should I Put My Money?

"Money is better than poverty, if only for financial reasons."
~Woody Allen

In February 2013, a California couple walking their dog along a path they had walked many times on their coastal property north of San Francisco noticed the edge of a rusty tin can poking up out of the dirt beside the trail. For reasons they could not explain later, they poked at the can and dug it out of the dirt. When they pried it open they found gold U.S. coins dated in the late 1880s. In the end, they dug up eight such cans worth an estimated $10 million.

The couple speculates that someone who worked in the mining industry received the coins as compensation and didn't trust banks. The person had stashed the money in sealed tin cans, intending perhaps to return some day and dig them up, but had probably died before he could do so. In all, over 1,400 gold coins were unearthed, all U.S. gold pieces originally worth around $30,000 — a small fortune for that time.

In Cleveland, Ohio, a contractor was remodeling a bathroom and found $182,000 in Depression-era currency hidden in a bathroom wall. The money had apparently been put there by the home's original owner, Patrick Dunne, a wealthy businessman who thought the wall would be a safer place for his cash than a bank. The money was minted in a time of bank collapses and joblessness. He probably reasoned that his cash was safer in the wall.

If you stop and think about it, there are only so many places to put your money:

- Banks (CDs, money market)
- Stocks
- Bonds
- Mutual funds
- Life insurance
- Your mattress
- Annuities
- Precious metals
- Real estate
- Currencies
- Commodities
- Collectibles

Can you think of any others? Other than bury it in tin cans or hide it in the walls, that is. There is no *wrong* place to put your money. There is also no *perfect* place to put your money. But there should be a *reason* why you put it where you do.

Knowing Your "Why"

We usually spend our first meeting working to understand our client's vision. The second thing we like to do when we take a case is to take a financial snapshot, so to speak. We like to spread everything out and see where clients have placed their assets and why. Only when you know where you are can you determine if you are on the right Retirement Highway.

All too often we discover that many don't know the "why" of their investments. One woman had several hundred thousand dollars in a variety of mutual funds.

"Why do you have these here?" we asked.

"I don't know," she replied.

During the last financial meltdown, we actually had a gentleman come into our office with bags of statements and all his assets in cash, seeking advice on where to put it. He said he distrusted the stock market and was afraid of banks.

It is essential that we know our "why" when it comes to investing. The decision of where to place your assets comes down to one key piece of information: What do you want it to do for you?

Why would you:

Buy stocks? Stocks can produce dividends, income, growth and profit. Yes, stocks come with a degree of risk, but even that can be mitigated if you invest properly in the stock market. A truly diversified stock portfolio can actually reduce risk.

Buy bonds? Security and safety. Government bonds are as secure as the government that issues them. Municipal bonds are as safe as the municipality. Corporate bonds are as secure as the corporation issuing them. But we are learning that bonds are not nearly as safe as they used to be. As of the time of this writing, the last bear market in bonds was in the mid-1980s. Stocks and bonds are sort of like opposing bookends. Bonds offer greater stability whereas stocks are more volatile. Bonds have an inverse relationship to interest rates. As a rule, when interest rates rise, bond values go down. Bonds have maturity dates. If you hold the bond until it matures, interest rates are a non-factor. Owning bonds for investment purposes, however, is another story. As we write this, interest rates have been very low for quite some time and can only go up.

Buy real estate? Well, for one thing, real estate is tangible. What you see is what you get. You can live on real estate (after all, you have to live somewhere). We used to believe that real estate values would always rise, didn't we? The housing crisis of 2007 taught a little lesson on that, though. Never assume anything when it comes to economic forces. Many who sank their money into real estate learned just how illiquid this investment can be. However, when prices bottom, if you have the disposable cash to invest, real estate can be an attractive investment. Just ask Donald Trump.

Buy commodities? Commodity prices (energy, metals, food, etc.) tend to move higher during periods of inflation. If you plan to own them long-term, commodities can provide an investor a hedge against inflation since they keep pace or exceed the inflation rate but there is risk involved. But beware: You can get burned.

Buy CDs? Most people buy CDs for safety and liquidity and they are not necessarily wrong on either count. Are CDs bulletproof? We had hundreds of banks fail in the last economic downturn. Why did the FDIC raise banks' insurance limit from $100,000 to $200,000? Because the government wanted banks to have a cushion. When the FDIC has to kick in and actually bail out a bank, the money comes out of the Federal Reserve, which comes out of our tax dollars, which comes out of our pockets. But the FDIC had to do it. Otherwise, a little pressure caused by another financial meltdown and a run on the banks could create chaos and another Great Depression.

Buy life insurance? The reason to buy life insurance is to protect our families. Some say that when you get past 65 you don't need life insurance anymore. "Our family is grown and gone," they say. "That's for young people to protect their families in case they die early." But did you know that you can use life insurance strategies to create modest returns tax-free and pass assets to the next generation in an efficient manner? Many today will openly say they believe taxes are going to be significantly higher in the future, but they inadvertently pass along a tax nightmare to their beneficiaries when they die by not investigating life insurance solutions.

The bigger you grow an IRA, the bigger tax time bomb you create. It might be more efficient to transfer some of that into a vehicle that can help ease that tax burden. You want your beneficiaries to have a pot of gold when you die, not a pile of taxes.

Buy annuities? You buy annuities for *income.* Some annuity salespeople will try to convince folks that annuities are like stocks, only without the risk. That is simply not true. You buy annuities for income now or income later, but you buy annuities for *income.* Annuities come under two main headings: immediate and deferred. When you get into deferred annuities, there are actually three subcategories to a deferred annuity.

(1) Fixed Annuities: These offer a simple fixed interest rate for a fixed period. A fixed annuity is like a CD with an insurance company instead of a bank. A fixed annuity is tax deferred instead of fully taxable.

(2) Variable Annuities: These are invested in stocks and mutual funds, so unlike fixed annuities, variable annuities can lose value. They have guarantees built into them, but watch out for the fees and other hidden charges.

(3) Fixed Index Annuities: These have safety and are guaranteed, and they have some upside potential. But don't let anyone compare them to investments, because they are not. They are meant to be a guaranteed asset with returns that are a little bit better than most other "safe" assets. They can do a great job if they are used properly.

The common denominator for all annuities is that they all are based on a contract with an insurance company. Thus, the guarantees that you hear about are only as firm as the insurance company backing the product. This is why it's important to check things like company ratings to be sure any annuity you consider is guaranteed by a strong, financially solvent insurer.

Many fixed index annuities are available with optional income riders, for which there is a fee. You can build an account with guaranteed growth and guaranteed income for later in life. Fixed index annuities can be a great source of income and a very important cog in the machinery of a portfolio.

Buy mutual funds? Investors purchase mutual funds mainly for diversification. Mutual funds were made for buy and hold investors. Like any at-risk position in the stock market, you have ups and downs. You may have a problem when you must pull income from a mutual fund when it is on a downward slide. The withdrawals make it retreat even further. The people who sold it to you may tell you thinks like, "Hang in there," or, "Don't worry, it will come back," or, "That's just the way these things work." Our opinion is that mutual funds are not the optimal vehicles for retirees to use for income. Besides that, many are expensive. You are paying for trading costs and management fees, and many are not aware that these fees are coming out of their account until they have them pointed out. Much of the returns of mutual funds are often lost to hidden fees lurking in the fine print of the prospectus.

Buy collectibles? Anything rare and unique should increase in value which can make them a good investment. Make sure you know what you're looking at before you purchase it. Antiques are not in our wheelhouse when it comes to investing, but common sense tells us that paying big money for some artifact without certification by an expert that it is genuine could be costly.

Pick Any Two

As we said earlier, there is no perfect place to put money. With banks you have safety and liquidity, but what do you *not* have? Good returns. With stocks you have good growth potential and liquidity, but in what area are they lacking? Safety. They contain risk. Real estate may be a good place for long-term growth and relative safety, but it is limited in liquidity. That point was proved to many investors in the harshest of terms after the housing bubble burst in 2007.

Wouldn't it be nice to have a place to put your money that would give you the following?

- Constant liquidity and easy accessibility
- A guaranteed high rate of return
- A rock-solid guarantee of safety where there was no chance of losing your principal

Would you do us a favor? When you find such an investment, would you please let us know about it? We have a waiting list of people who are interested, ourselves included!

On the occasions when we have the time for a road trip on our Harleys, we love to take to the back roads. On one such trip, we stopped at a small country store in a rural area of North Carolina. On the wall above the cash register was an unforgettable sign that read: "Good Service. Low Prices. High Quality. — Pick Any Two." Maybe you have seen the sign before, but it was a first for us. The inference is obvious for a country store. Who wouldn't be willing to pay a few cents extra for the items in this mom and pop grocery store just to soak in the atmosphere of a genuine country store that offers a little bit of everything and not too much of anything?

It's the same way with investing. You are unlikely to find an investment with perfect liquidity, high returns and absolute safety of principal. More often than not, you will shave a few points off one of those cardinal attributes to obtain what you need of the others. That's where proper planning comes in. Knowing specifically what you want your money to accomplish for you is half the battle in selecting the proper place to put it.

Ken Heise sits astride his ride in Montana for the Harley 100th anniversary ride.

CHAPTER 7

Staying on the Right Retirement Highway with Your Investments

"Here's how I think of my money - as soldiers - I send them out to war every day. I want them to take prisoners and come home, so there's more of them." ~ Kevin O'Leary

M aybe you've heard a conversation such as this, perhaps in the office coffee room, when Joe, the self-proclaimed stock market genius walks in and offers his latest "hot tip" on what could be the next Microsoft or Google:

"I'm only letting a few people in on this," Joe says, and proceeds to tell you about a startup company that has technology that will revolutionize online shopping. "But you got to get in while it's hot," warns Joe. "This thing is going to *explode!"*

What's wrong with this picture? First, it sounds too good to be true, and that means it usually is. Secondly, there is no way to *measure* the behavior of this investment, is there? The company is a startup. It has no history. You could lose everything you invest if it turns out that Joe is wrong and this company does not have a lock on the technology, or the technology is flawed, or if another company beats them to the market with the same idea. Any number of things could go wrong. Of course, there is an outside chance that Joe could be right but this is not investing; it's betting on a long shot.

But what about other investment opportunities that aren't so obvious? Is there a way to analyze them to weigh the risk versus reward? What about holdings within our portfolio? Is there a tool with which we may measure their risk/reward quotient?

The *Retirement Roadmap Review*®

P.A.T.H. is an acronym for Planning Assessment Thoroughly and Holistically. The "assessment" part of it involves taking a financial snapshot to determine if your assets are properly positioned according to your stated financial goals. The *Retirement Roadmap Review*® involves a thorough **risk analysis** to determine if your investments are in harmony with your risk tolerance and whether they are age-appropriate. Our observation is that the portfolios of many seniors are too heavy on the risk side of the risk/reward equation.

Risk analysis can be a real eye-opener for some. We often hear expressions like, "You've got to be kidding me!" and "I had no idea!" A conservative estimate is that at least half of the people we sit down with for a *Retirement Roadmap Review*® have no idea of the risk they are taking with their investments until we do the analysis.

Perhaps you have heard the old story that illustrates the difference between knowledge, understanding and wisdom. It goes like this: Knowledge is the collection of facts. If a man is standing in the middle of a railroad track, he has **knowledge** of the basic fact of where he is. He also knows that a train is coming. Those are facts.

He understands the relationship of his soft tissue to the hard steel of the locomotive, and he has an **understanding** of the velocity of the train and the impact a collision could have on his person.

Wisdom is getting off the track.

Why is it that so many people don't know their risk quotient? Because the brokers who call themselves financial advisors don't advise them sufficiently of the downside potential. Have you ever had a conversation with your advisor that goes like this?

You: "I have all these things in my portfolio here...Can you give me a rough idea of what I might expect to lose if we have another meltdown like the one we had in 2008?"

Advisor: "Well, based on what I see, you are in a position to lose about half of your life's savings. If you're okay with that, then I guess you are fine!"

No, we doubt that you will ever have a conversation like that. Most people who sell stocks for a living are quick to tell their prospects how much they stand to gain but are slow to point out how much they can lose. This is one of the reasons we developed the *Retirement Roadmap Review*® system of financial planning. Market volatility is a fact of modern investing. Market crashes happen. We can no more control them than we can control the weather. But just because we can't control the rain doesn't mean that we have to be caught out in it. No one should be subjected to the horror of watching half of their life savings go down the drain because they either listened to the wrong advice or failed to receive the right advice.

Standard Deviation Analysis

Standard deviation and variance are mathematical terms. Deviation just means *"how far from normal."* Standard deviation is simply the measure of *"how spread out numbers are."*

It makes sense that the more a stock's returns vary from the stock's average return, the more volatile the stock. Check out the two stocks below, stock A and stock B. Look at the total average return and then notice the final dollar amounts at the end of the observation period. Did you notice that both stocks averaged returns of 1.43 percent? Yet, look at stock A's individual returns. It has much higher highs but much lower lows. That is an example of a volatile stock. Stock A's range is from negative nine percent to plus 12 percent, while Stock B ranges from zero to three percent. That "average" may be the same, but Standard Deviation measures all the values. The standard deviation of the six returns for Stock A is **8.8**; for stock B it is **1.27**. If you are trying to make your holding *safer* and less risky, which stock would you choose to own and which stock would you choose to eliminate from your portfolio?

Compare Two Products Assuming $1,000 Initial Investment			
Stock A		Stock B	
Return	$	Return	$
-9	$910	2	$1,020
6	$965	3	$1,051
-5	$916	0	$1,051
12	$1,026	3	$1,082
8	$1,108	1	$1,093
-9	$1,009	0	$1,093
7	$1,079	1	$1,104
Average	1.42%	Average	1.42%
Std Dev	8.8	Std Dev	1.27

But wait a minute! Both averaged the same amount!

Yes, that's true. But one is more predictable and less likely to be affected by the variances of the market than the other. You want solid and secure, not explosive and dangerous when you are in the preservation and distribution phases of your financial lives.

When it comes to standard deviation analysis, remember these two simple facts:

- There are scientific ways to measure the risk factor of stocks. That is much better than going on human intuition, or how you *feel* about certain investments.
- If you are retiring, we feel strongly that you should make the securities portion of your portfolio safer, not riskier.

No formula can perfectly predict future returns. A stock that has been consistent for years could experience sudden, sharp fluctuations. But standard deviation analysis helps us invest intelligently and respond appropriately to market forces we can't control.

Dispersion

A term frequently used in this type of risk analysis is "dispersion." In ordinary speech, the word "dispersion" means *"the scattering or distribution of something within an area or space."* But when we are dealing with statistical analysis, it refers to the size of the range of values expected for a particular variable. In finance, a large dispersion tells us how much the return on the investment is deviating from the expected normal returns. When you measure anything, you must have a standard. When you are dealing with securities, the standard of expectations is often an index, such as the S&P index. When measuring the performance of a mutual fund, for example, fund managers will often measure the returns against the S&P index, which is widely regarded as a benchmark. If the dispersion, or range of values, is greater than that of the benchmark, then the investment is probably riskier. If the dispersion is less, then the investment is less risky. The smaller the dispersion measure, the more consistent the returns should be.

On one analysis we did, a man had a $1 million portfolio parked with a stock broker but wasn't sure what his overall return was. He told his broker that he needed only a five percent return on his money. He said that if he had a five percent return, he could pay bills and live a reasonably comfortable life.

When we did the analysis, we discovered that his portfolio was averaging a 10 percent return! The man was very pleased. This broker is a guru! A stock market whiz!

Hold the phone. That wasn't the entire picture. The portfolio was loaded with risk. It was like a speeding train heading for a curve in the track. The standard deviation analysis revealed that this man's portfolio was a financial disaster waiting to happen. The man would have found that out if he had waited until the next stock market meltdown. We estimated that his losses if another 2008-type market crash occurred would be about $440,000. He was able to reposition his assets based on a return closer to six percent. Now, with the lower standard deviation number, if he experienced a 2008-type market crash he would only lose $120,000 of his $1 million portfolio.

Other Aspects of the *Retirement Roadmap Review*®

A *Retirement Roadmap Review*® allows the financial advisor to (a) fully understand what the client's goals and objectives are; (b) lay them side by side with his or her current placement of assets;

and (c) create a plan that makes them match. We have already discussed STEP ONE, *risk review.* STEP TWO is *fee discovery.*

Many people are shocked to discover the true cost of their mutual funds, stocks and other investments. Have you ever discovered that you were being intentionally overcharged? How did it make you feel? Victimized? Betrayed? Abused? All of the above? We don't blame you. We think it is vital to have a complete awareness of every fee and every charge associated with your investment accounts. Each unnecessary dollar you are paying out in fees could instead be working for you and protecting you financially in retirement. We like to "pull back the curtain" on some of these egregious over-chargers and run the money-changers out of the temple, so to speak. A subsequent chapter in this book will specifically deal with those on the "most-wanted list." Fine print on your statement is there for a reason, you know.

STEP THREE of the *Retirement Roadmap Review*® process is developing an income plan that perfectly fits how clients envision their individual retirement. No two people are exactly alike. It is impossible to stamp out financial plans assembly line-style as if one size fits all. Financial plans are as individual as fingerprints — no two are exactly alike, not even with identical twins. To illustrate the point, you could take two people who are the same age, live across the street from each other, work at the same job, have the same income and same size family, the same net worth and the same investments and they would have (or should have) different financial plans. Why? Because their goals and values are not the same. Wealth means different things to each of them. You will learn more about this in a subsequent chapter dealing with an inflation-adjusted laddered income plan that is designed to ensure retirees that their financial wellspring doesn't run dry in retirement.

STEP FOUR of the *Retirement Roadmap Review*® process deals with the estate. In each of the steps, we make sure that we look at the "whole" financial life and plan with the entire financial picture in mind. That's what the word holistic means. In the practice of holistic medicine, everything is considered — body, mind, spirit and emotions. The idea is that one affects the rest, and they all affect each other. It does no good to treat one area and ignore another. Under the heading "What is Holistic Medicine," WebMD says the following:

"Holistic medicine practitioners believe that the whole person is made up of interdependent parts and if one part is not working properly, all the other parts will be affected. In this way, if people have imbalances (physical, emotional, or spiritual) in their lives, it can negatively affect their overall health...

"For example, when a person suffering from migraine headaches pays a visit to a holistic doctor...the doctor will likely take a look at all the potential factors that may be causing the person's headaches, such as other health problems, diet and sleep habits, stress and personal problems, and preferred spiritual practices. The treatment plan may involve drugs to relieve symptoms, but also lifestyle modifications to help prevent the headaches from recurring.","[8]

Likewise, a competent financial advisor will look at more than just the client's personal finances but will want to ensure that the client's wishes regarding family are carried out to the letter. Most people want their family protected. They want such documents as wills, trusts, powers of attorney, advance medical directives, etc. to harmonize and accurately reflect their wishes. A simple thing such as properly named beneficiaries can make thousands of dollars' worth of difference to the family members you leave behind.

Most people we know are good Americans. They like Uncle Sam; they just don't want to adopt him into their family and make him the beneficiary of their estate. Most people we know don't mind paying their fair share of taxes, but they resent having to pay

---

[8] WebMD. "What Is Holistic Medicine?"
https://www.webmd.com/balance/guide/what-is-holistic-medicine#1

one penny **more** than their fair share. Another portion of this fourth step of our *Retirement Roadmap Review*® is to find every nickel of unnecessary taxes you may be paying and put it back in your estate, not the government's coffers.

The Heise family at a family get-together in 2015.

CHAPTER 8

The Hidden Fees in Mutual Funds

We live in a world of fees. Take traveling as an example. If you go to the airport, there are fees to park your car. If you have the audacity to travel with luggage, there is an extra fee to check your bags. If you check your bags out front, there is a fee for that. That's right, a fee to pay a fee. Once you are on the plane you can have a sandwich and a bag of pretzels for a fee. A wireless internet connection is available for a fee. Remember the free in-flight movies? Now they charge for the cheap headphones you need to watch it. As I write this, there is no charge for using the restrooms, but it wouldn't surprise me if that were next. We understand why these fees exist, of course. Times are tough for the airlines, and they need to raise revenue without raising ticket prices. That still doesn't make them any more palatable.

Times must be tough for the banking industry, too. Remember free checking? These days, unless you keep a few thousand dollars in there, there is a fee for every conceivable banking transaction.

Most egregious are the fees that blindside you. When you make your hotel reservation, you are quoted a rate. You negotiate the rate (there is usually haggle room here) and you fully expect that rate will be what you pay. Then, upon checking out, you discover there is a fee for that bottle of water you thought was a courtesy of the management. There is another fee for the outside calls you made. There may also be "resort fees" and "concierge fees," which is hotel talk for charging you still more for services you thought were included.

The reason we resent hidden fees more than those that are out in the open is because we feel tricked and betrayed. We feel as if we have been taken to the cleaners and artfully robbed. It assaults our sense of fairness.

Hidden Fees in Mutual Funds

You can't get something for nothing, as the saying goes, and investing is no different. No matter what products or companies you use, there will be some kind of cost, whether it is a commission or fee or tax, etc. Yet, there are two important things we want to know when it comes to what we pay: 1. How much are we paying? And 2. Are we getting enough value for what we pay for?

If we don't know and understand number one, we cannot hope to answer number two. Unfortunately, when it comes to investment products — in particular, mutual funds — it isn't easy to know how much you are paying. Some people think of this unseen drain as a landmine; you don't know it's there until it is too late. We think of them more in the vein of a parasite, like a tapeworm on your finances. You don't know it's there, and you may not recognize its effects, but it's draining your mutual fund of its earning power and potential. No matter what colorful predatory images you want to use, the bottom line is this: any fees drain your portfolio of its energy and potential. Check out the effect of even these comparatively low fees on a portfolio over time:

Now, those are fees we can see. But what about the fees we can't, the ones lurking under the surface and draining your portfolio from within? One very popular product has a particular reputation for hidden fees: the mutual fund. In fact, "very popular" is an understatement. In 2017, reports from various product sales showed that mutual funds are the most popular investing product out there, with 45 percent of all U.S. households owning mutual funds in some form—56 million households.[9]

---

[9] Bernice Napach. Think Advisor. Oct. 13, 2017. "Why Mutual Funds Are the Most Popular Investment for US Households: ICI."
http://www.thinkadvisor.com/2017/10/13/why-mutual-funds-are-the-most-popular-investment-f.

Why are mutual funds so popular? For one thing, they are an easy way to diversify. Since each fund can own portions of numerous companies, they aren't as volatile as owning stock in one or two companies. For another thing, since mutual funds are usually actively managed by a team of professionals, it allows investors to have hands-on management without having to be a gazillionaire-level client in a steel-and-glass covered firm. Of course, one big piece of mutual fund popularity is that they are a fixture in the majority of employer-sponsored retirement plans (401(k)s and IRAs.

If you are one of those mutual fund owners, it's likely you've at least heard of the "expense ratio," even if you can't cite verbatim what yours is. The expense ratio is the annual fee that a mutual fund charges its shareholder, the percentage of your assets that are deducted each year for the disclosed asset-based cost of your mutual fund.

The costs disclosed in your expense ratio are what we call "stated costs." They are in your fund prospectus, which is likely a giant stack of papers you get every year from the mutual fund company. Stated costs are the above-the-surface costs, and include the following:

- Administrative fees: This is the fee the fund may charge in order to pay for day-to-day operations of the firm that operates the mutual fund.
- Marketing fees: Mutual funds are highly competitive. To attract investors, some of the top management firms spend millions in advertising and paying reviewers, bloggers and economists to hype their product. The cost of such marketing is then passed to—you guessed it—the investors.
- Management fees: Actively managed funds will, of course, have fund managers. Competition can be fierce, and the companies that package mutual funds often pay

handsomely to recruit and retain talent. Again, the cost for that management is passed on to consumers.

- Loads: It's likely that the financial advisor you work with, whether your advisor is independent or part of a big brokerage, is getting paid for recommending the mutual fund. When talking about mutual fund loads, we basically are talking about commissions. A front-loaded fund is a mutual fund where the commission is taken out before your money is ever invested. If you want to invest $10,000 in a mutual fund with a two percent front-end load, you'll need to start your investment out at $10,200 to be able to pay the load and still invest what you wanted. Back-end loads are the opposite; a fund with a back-end load means you will pay your financial professional's commission when you are withdrawing funds.

Again, all of the preceding costs are included in the expense ratio. They are known, quantified costs. Unfortunately, like iceberg tips, the expense ratios, the known costs, give you no indication of how large the total berg may be once you dip beneath the icy surface. A quick Google search may give you an idea of what we're talking about—with titles such as "The Hidden Costs of Investing in Mutual Funds," "Beware the Hidden Costs of Mutual Funds," and "Uncovering Hidden Costs of Mutual Fund Investing," it becomes clear that the costs that loom beneath the surface of your fund's prospectus are no secret.

How do we get these lurking, unstated costs? They surely affect your portfolio as much as the stated costs—after all, fees are fees. The range of unstated costs that may be draining your portfolio are the transactional costs on the actual stock portions inside the mutual fund. While you might own a few shares of the mutual fund, each mutual fund is made up of a number of stocks from other companies, and those stocks have their own costs, such as:

- Trading costs: When your mutual fund's manager buys and sells stock from inside the fund, that has its own cost. Mutual funds that have more trades, more stocks being bought and sold at any given time, will have more of these costs, costs which may never be disclosed to mutual fund shareholders.

- Trading commissions: Just like trading costs, these costs are inherent to a mutual fund in that, when fund managers buy and sell the stocks in a fund, they are paid a commission on those sales. Again, the higher the turnover in a fund, the more likely it is that a fund shareholder is losing ground quietly, due to paying an unknown amount in commissions.

- Market impact costs: Stock sales in and out of mutual funds aren't happening in a vacuum; they are subject to the whims and tides of the market, as well. Market impact costs are basically the potential cost the fund incurs from buying or selling at the less-than-optimal time or in a less-than-optimal quantity. Unfavorable market circumstances will still affect your mutual fund shares but won't ever make it into your expense ratio for full disclosure.

- Taxes: One of the biggest unstated costs of a mutual fund is the annual expense of taxes. If your shares are held in a taxable account, you are required to pay taxes on any dividends your fund made in that year—even if the dividends were reinvested. If the mutual fund manager moves you between shares in one fund to another, you will pay capital gains tax. And if the mutual fund manager sells a stock at a profit that has been held in the fund for less than a year, you could have to pay short-term capital gains tax (which is taxed at your ordinary income tax rate) on that gain, even if your mutual fund shares actually LOST value overall that year.

Many of these costs are something you can guess at based on your mutual fund's turnover, or the amount of its assets that it sells and replaces in any given year. An average small-cap stock fund has an average turnover of 90 percent, meaning it replaces nearly all of its assets in any given year. Remember, all those trades and replacements have costs and commissions. If 90 percent replacement is the *average,* can you imagine a fund with 140 percent annual turnover?[10]

Performance

Of course, all these aforementioned costs are only relevant insofar as they help answer "Am I getting what I pay for?" Unfortunately, measuring mutual fund performance isn't easy. For one thing, as with all stock-based investments, past performance is no indicator of future results; what did well yesterday might tank tomorrow, or vice versa.

While many people invest in mutual funds based on some sort of rating such as Morningstar's one-to-five-star scale, those stars can only tell you how a mutual fund did in the past, not how they might perform in the future. Another difficult thing about discovering the performance of a fund is what some call "survivorship bias," meaning that funds that fail and collapse are often not counted in mutual fund performance. This is pretty significant considering that Morningstar reported in 2014 that 40 percent of traditional U.S. mutual funds operating in 2004 shut

[10] Kent Thune. The Balance. Aug. 31, 2017. "What is Turnover Ratio?" https://www.thebalance.com/what-is-turnover-ratio-2466651.

down by 2014. That included 20 percent of five-star-rated funds. But those underperforming funds won't show up in historical data measuring mutual fund successes, making it difficult to measure mutual fund performance across the board.[11]

Are They a Good Investment?

When you take a snapshot at the world of investing from 30,000 feet up, a vast landscape appears and the options are endless. Are mutual funds a good investment? The answer has to be "it depends." It depends on age, circumstances, financial goals and the extent to which you wish to be personally involved in the flow of your invested cash. Mutual funds certainly have their place in this vast landscape, otherwise they wouldn't exist and otherwise they would not be the repository of so many billions of dollars. The real question is: are they a good investment for you? The answer to that is complex and multidimensional. It requires analysis on several levels which we are always happy to provide.

---

[11] Larry Swedroe. MoneyWatch. May 8, 2014. "How the Mutual Fund Graveyard Can Hurt Investors." https://www.cbsnews.com/news/its-getting-crowded-in-the-mutual-fund-graveyard/.

*Several Heise family members gather in November 2017 at Camp Randall Stadium
in Wisconsin to cheer on the Badgers football team.*

CHAPTER 9

The Inflation Laddering Income Plan

"When I was 40, my doctor advised me that a man in his forties shouldn't play tennis. I heeded his advice carefully and could hardly wait until I reached 50 to start again." ~ Hugo L. Black

An individual who eventually became a client of ours came in for a *Retirement Roadmap Review®*. We will call him Jeff. Jeff had a $500,000 portfolio and was taking out $20,000 per year on the advice of his financial advisor at the brokerage house where his money was invested. Why that amount? The broker was adhering to what is called in the financial community as the "Four Percent Withdrawal Rule," an antiquated investing formula which basically asserts that a retiree can withdraw four percent per year from a market-based investment account and never run out of money.

Things were going along just fine for Jeff until 2008, when the troubles on Wall Street came to a boil. The aftershocks of what economists now call the "Financial Crisis of 2008" caused Jeff to lose almost half of his life's savings virtually overnight. Painfully, Jeff learned quickly that you can't spend a percent.

What would happen if you worked for a corporation and one morning you arrived at your office for work and the manager asked to have a word with you in private? You know something is coming, right?

"We value you highly and we appreciate your work," says the manager. "But we are going to cut your pay by 50 percent." What would you do? You would probably look for another job, right?

It should be the same with our retirement investments. Jeff's living expenses were not cut in half. He did have other income from his Social Security and a small pension, but he still needed his lifestyle. That meant that he would now have to withdraw eight percent per year. Now how long would his resources last? Jeff was not at all satisfied with the broker's answer: "Just hang in there," he was told. "It will all come back."

"That would have been acceptable 10 years ago," Jeff complained. "But I am in withdrawal mode here."

The question in Jeff's mind is obvious. How long is his money going to last now that his investment account has lost half its value *and* now that he is forced to withdraw twice as much percentage-wise as before? Yes, the market will rebound, but will his account have enough time to rebound with it?

Investing in the 21st Century

Investing strategies should have an expiration date stamped on them, just like a carton of milk. What used to work to our advantage when we were in our salaried working days may not work to our advantage once we approach retirement. We must rethink our entire strategy. Our mission when we approach retirement is to preserve and protect our resources and create an income that will sustain us throughout retirement. Job one is to prevent the erosion of principal. In farming, there is a time to plant and there is a time to reap. There is a time to store the produce of the fields and preserve it for winter. It's the same in investing: We must change tactics when the purpose of our investing changes.

Is it possible to provide a guaranteed income while at the same time withdrawing money from an asset account? Won't draining the account for the purposes of income reduce the principal? Not necessarily. Bengen was spot on trying to create a formula that would allow withdrawals from the account while preserving the account for life. There are still ways to do that, but not with the precepts of the "Four Percent Withdrawal Rule." The way to do it is through a concept known as "Laddering."

Laddering calls for dividing your assets into what we call "time categories." Laddering allows you to generate a paycheck in retirement without severely eroding your principal. We are particularly fond of a strategy known as ILIP, which stands for Inflation Laddering Income Plan.

Note that inflation is the first word in ILIP. That's because we are talking about a *lifetime* income plan here. How long will you live in retirement? You don't know. But from an actuarial point of view, if you are in good health, the chances of your retirement lasting 20 years are excellent. Your chances are very good that it could last as many as 30 years. Inflation is a factor in producing a lifetime income. You may establish a strategy for producing an income, but if that income comes up short, then you have aimed too low. The challenge is to guarantee an income that is both long lasting and one that compensates for the steady pressure of inflation to erode the buying power of the dollar. The last thing you want to do is lock into an income stream, only to find out 10 or 15 years hence that it can no longer support your lifestyle. What would you do then? Returning to work is one option, true. After that long a layoff, it may not be possible and, even if it were, it likely would not be desirable. If you resume working after retirement, you want to do it because you enjoy it, not because you are forced into it by unwise decisions you made prior to retirement.

Effects of Inflation

People of the baby boom generation remember buying gasoline for under 50 cents per gallon. According to Hemmings Daily, a newsletter for classic car aficionados, the sticker price for a 1965 V-8 Ford Mustang was $2,734, and the average production worker making $3.00 per hour would have to work 911 hours, or 23 weeks, to pay cash for the car. In 2013 the equivalent car cost $31,545 and requires that a worker earning $27.15 per hour put in 1,162 hours to pay for it. Any way you look at it, inflation has eaten away the value of the dollar and at the balance of what we pay for what we get.

According to Ask.com, a 1965 loaf of bread cost 21 cents, a candy bar cost 5 cents and milk was 95 cents per gallon. The U.S. Bureau of Labor Statistics has a nifty little calculator on their website that lets you see just how much the dollar's buying power has eroded over the years. We plugged in a number at random - $50,000 — and picked a random year, 1987, and let the computer tell us how much buying power would be needed in 2014 to equal it. Would you believe $144,625.61? In other words, had you locked into an income of $50,000 in 1987 you would need to have almost triple that amount 27 years later to buy the same goods and services. Think of that in terms of rent, food, gasoline, medicine. It is easy to see how inflation can affect your retirement if you let it. [12]

---

[12] Bureau of Labor Statistics. CPI Inflation Calculator.
https://www.bls.gov/data/inflation_calculator.htm.

Some investors focus on higher returns. After all, if inflation averages three percent per year and you can average 10 percent per year, that leaves seven percent to the good. Problem solved, right? Not really. First, we don't know of anyone who has experienced a steady 10 percent return on their market investments over a protracted period. Second, there is no guarantee. What if your portfolio loses money?

Why is it that the S&P 500 index averaged 6.95% from 2006-2016 but the average investor in the stock market netted only a 3.64% return? Because emotions get in the way.[13] The mantra of investing in the market (investing in anything, for that matter) has always been, "Buy low; sell high." If the stock market behaved predictably and the line were a straight diagonal from point A to point B instead of a zigzag, then all would be rosy. But the market doesn't behave that way when emotions are involved. You lose 30 percent, the market bounces back and you gain 40 percent. Just when you are feeling great about your investing savvy, the bottom drops out and you lose 40 percent. You reason the market will bounce back like before, but this time it is slow going. You vow that you will hold on until you get back to square one, but when the market recovers again, you hold on longer knowing there is profit just around the corner. And sure enough, there is! You hold on a little too long, however, and your position retraces. Now you are in selling mode just at the wrong time. As soon as you get out of the position, the market climbs back and you miss out on the rally. So the market may gain 10 percent over a 20-year period but the average investor sells on the way down and buys on the way up out of fear or greed. Human emotions seem to trump averages

---

[13] James Picerno. Seeking Alpha. Sept. 21, 2017. "Investor Returns Vs. Market Returns: The Failure Endures." https://seekingalpha.com/article/4108688-investor-returns-vs-market-returns-failure-endures

because of the inherent volatility and unpredictability of the market.

The Emotional Cycle of Investing

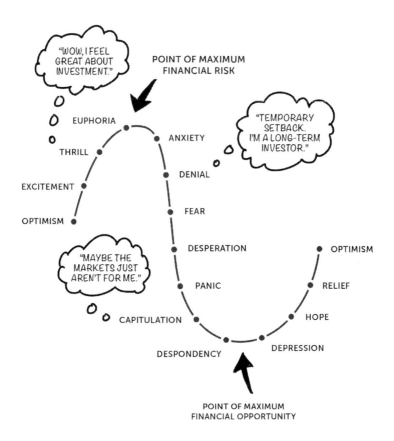

Pick a Number and Plan for It

In doing research for this book we discovered a helpful website, www.usinflationcalculator.com, which gives you a table of historical inflation rates by month and year going all the way back to 1914. It is put out by Coin News, a newsletter for numismatists (coin collectors) and they reference the Consumer Price Index (CPI) and the U.S. Bureau of Labor Statistics as resources. We were surprised to see how out of control Inflation was from 1917-1920. The inflation rate peaked at 17.4 percent in 1917. That was followed by a period of deflation. In 1921, for example, prices for goods and services actually dropped 10.5 percent while the currency found its footing and stabilized for a number of years after that. The year of hyper-inflation was 1980 when the rate jumped to 13.5 percent. The website's calculator shows that if you had retired in 1988 expecting to live on $50,000, you would need double that in 2014 to maintain the same lifestyle. That means that the **cumulative** rate of inflation during that 26-year span was just over 100 percent.[14]

Planning for inflation requires us to pick a number. How much will the inflation rate be over the next 30 years? We don't know. But a look back in history can tell us what it has been in the past 30 years. Many baby boomers remember the period of hyper-inflation they lived through in the late 1970s and early 1980s when Jimmy Carter was president and mini-skirts and polyester leisure suits were in style. Could that happen again? It could. There is no way to know. So how do you plan? You pick a likely number given what we know from past data and use it. As we write this, the current inflation rate is 2.2 percent, but we are in a period of low inflation. We feel a good, safe number to use for planning purposes is three percent.

Pick another number — your monthly living expenses. Let's say $5,000 per month is the magic number there. You need $60,000 per year in annual income for food, clothing, shelter, transportation and taxes, and that will give you a little left over for such things as occasional travel and eating out. What will that

---

[14] US Inflation Calculator. "Historical Inflation Rates: 1914-2018."
http://www.usinflationcalculator.com/inflation/historical-inflation-rates/.

$5,000 per month need to be in five years? Ten years? Fifteen years? Twenty years? Using our three percent inflation, we come up with:

5 years - $5,796.37
10 years - $6,719.58
15 years - $7,789.84
20 years - $9,030.55

Unless you want to pare down your standard of living, you will need to have a plan to make up for that shortfall.

The ILIP Plan in Action

Laddering is an income planning technique which can be likened to the way airplanes store and distribute fuel to the engines. Charles Lindberg would never have been able to make his historic first flight across the Atlantic Ocean if he hadn't planned his fuel very carefully. The Spirit of St. Louis would carry 450 gallons of fuel in five tanks. The plane was heavy on take-off and barely made it over the trees at the end of a muddy runway. Once Lindberg was airborne, he had to switch the fuel tanks at intervals to balance out the weight since the wing tanks carried one-third of the plane's fuel.

If you want to make your nest egg last throughout your retirement, you must plan. Put your assets in several "buckets," each with its own strategic purpose. The end goal is to make your resources last the rest of your life **and** accommodate anticipated inflation.

Joe and Susan have a nest egg of $1,175,000. They want to guarantee themselves a $2,500 per month income which, in addition to their monthly Social Security check, allows them to meet basic expenses and maintain their current lifestyle. This income — and this is important — should also have a built-in adjustment for inflation. They put $525,000 into "income buckets" where they have decent growth but cannot lose their principal. The rest of their nest egg, $650,000, they put into accounts that have a degree of risk but a greater potential for growth.

What does that do? The "income buckets" guarantee them a pension-like income that they cannot outlive. Bucket one gives them a $2,500 per month income for one year. Bucket two provides a $2,600 monthly paycheck for them in years 2-6. Bucket 3 kicks in during year seven with $3,000 per month for the rest of the lives. All of this from the $525,000.

What about the $650,000 they didn't use for income? They put this money to work for them in investments that have a degree of risk lower than they would have assumed during their working years. Call it the "Investment Bucket," since it is designed for (a) liquidity and (b) growth. This is where you might have investments such as preferred stocks, bonds, Real Estate Investment Trusts (REITS), and other investments that produce high yields and dividends. This bucket, because of its growth potential, is also a hedge against inflation. The $3,000 per month Joe and Susan have coming in from "income bucket" three will probably not be enough at some point in their retirement. Inflation will have whittled its buying power down. So where do they turn to make up for the shortfall? Their "investment bucket!"

The three "income buckets" are set up differently. Joe and Susan fund bucket one with $30,000 for one year's worth of income. They fund bucket two with $150,000 for five years of income. They fund bucket three with $345,000 for a guaranteed lifetime income. When Joe and Susan pass away, any money left in bucket three will transfer to their beneficiaries. Keep in mind, while these buckets are feeding Joe and Susan monthly paychecks, they are, at the same time, positioning assets for growth. If Joe and

Susan die 20 years after they start the laddering income plan, they would have received a total of $690,000 in income from their "income buckets," the accounts which are principal protected. Meanwhile, if the investment bucket earned only five percent interest over 20 years, it would have grown to $1,173,972! If Joe and Susan had been able to live on what the "income buckets" provided and had not touched the "investment bucket," under that scenario it would be passed on as a legacy to their beneficiaries.

Strategic Income Planning

When Lindberg landed the Spirit of St. Louis at Le Bourget Field in Paris on May 21, 1927 he had plenty of fuel left in his tanks. As soon as his monoplane touched down, he was mobbed by reporters. They asked him if he had any concerns about not having enough fuel to make it to Paris. Lindberg told them no. He had plenty of fuel. In fact, he said he felt sure he could have flown another 1,000 miles if it were necessary.

One reason Lindberg could be so confident of having enough fuel to make the trip successfully is because he was such a meticulous planner. He left nothing to chance. He calculated every ounce he took with him on his historic flight, even to the point that he refused to carry with him a change of clothes or more than three letters. Every ounce of weight represented that much fuel he couldn't carry.

The more attention we give to planning our income for retirement, the more carefree and enjoyable it can be for us. There are those who continue the "accumulation style" of investing when they are in the "preservation and distribution" phases of their financial lives. When they should be enjoying the sound of the surf on some white, sandy beach, they are likely worrying about what the stock market is doing. When you use strategies that are contractually guaranteed, you will have the confidence of knowing how you are going to finance the lifestyle and you can just enjoy living life.

Our advice is not to go it alone, but to find trained financial professionals who specialize in retirement income planning and can select just the right strategies for you — the strategies that meet your unique circumstances, risk tolerances and goals. There is nothing quite like the peace of mind that comes from knowing exactly where your next paycheck is coming from in retirement and that it will be enough to meet your needs.

*The Heise's grandson, Hayden, takes a moment
to snuggle their granddaughter, Gabriella.*

CHAPTER 10

Protect Your Assets from Market Risk

"The most successful businessperson is the one who holds onto the old just as long as it is good and grabs the new just as soon as it is better." ~ Robert P. Vanderpoel

Free market economies are sometimes capable of strange behavior. When we examine with 20/20 hindsight the events that led up to the stock market crash of 2008, we can't help but scratch our heads and wonder how things could have gotten so out of hand. Market analysts are still debating whether it was the fault of greedy bankers or a failure on the part of government regulators. We are left with the impression that markets seem to have a mind all their own and cannot be controlled, only observed. Bubbles like the tech bubble of 2000 and the housing market bubble of 2007 seem to materialize and feed on themselves until they burst, causing panic on Wall Street and shattered portfolios.

Since no one can predict when and how such phenomena will happen, it is up to investors, especially those entering their retirement years, to be vigilant and protect the assets they have worked and saved so arduously from the volatility of a restless and unpredictable market.

The Tulip Bubble of 1637

The earliest example of an economic bubble affecting the world's economy is the "tulip bubble" of 1637. As bizarre as it sounds, tulips became a sort of currency when people in the Netherlands began trading them as if they were commodities. It all started when tulips, which were indigenous to Turkey, were introduced to Europe in the late 1500s. Europeans found the tulip exotically beautiful and strangely appealing. It soon became fashionable for rich people to have massive tulip gardens of red, yellow and pink gracing their mansions. Amsterdam merchants, who were at the center of the East Indies trade, caught onto the fact that they could make a boatload of money selling tulip bulbs. It was a craze for which there was no logical explanation, but people just wanted them and were willing to pay exorbitant prices for them.

One factor that contributed to the value of tulip bulbs was the length of time it took for a seed to grow into a bulb - seven to 12 years. Some bulbs were rare because they produced multi-colored tulips. These bulbs were highly sought after — the law of supply and demand at work.

Speculators entered the market buying up supplies of bulbs hoping to make a profit. They sold them to other traders who had no interest in the flowers themselves but just wanted to find a buyer. It was apparent that the inflated bulb prices had nothing to do with demand for the flowers but was a manifestation of greed on the part of the speculators. The bubble reached its bursting point when tulip traders couldn't find enough buyers. That's when the panic began. Tulip traders scrambled to unload their bulbs, and the prices fell precipitously. Some were left holding bulbs they had paid for with borrowed money and lost everything they had. "Tulip deflation" started in the Netherlands and soon spread to all of Europe, affecting the economies of all the civilized world in one way or another.

Keeping Your Nest Egg Safe

A point we have made often in this book is that how you invested when you were 35 is not how you should invest when you are 65. The investing strategies that got you to retirement are not the same strategies that will get you through retirement. When you approach retirement, you are no longer in the accumulation phase of your financial life; you are in the preservation and distribution phase and each phase calls for a different investing strategy.

No one — repeat, no one — can accurately foretell the future when it comes to investing. We anticipate that sooner or later there will be another market crash. That is the cyclical nature of the market. Standard deviation analysis calls for understanding that markets are capable of wide swings. The gentleman we met in chapter seven with a $1 million portfolio was experiencing high returns but was at too much risk according to his own risk tolerance. He could not afford to lose as much as half of his life's savings in another market correction. So, with an adjustment to his standard deviation to reduce the overall risk of his portfolio, he knew that if he woke up one morning to learn that the market had nose-dived, his portfolio, although it may lose a little, wouldn't go down in flames.

Would Your Life Change If...

A question we like to ask when we are building a *Retirement Roadmap Review*® in our office at Heise Advisory Group is: "Would your life change significantly if you were to experience a 50 percent gain in your portfolio?" Most people say no. Their lifestyle is their chosen lifestyle. They may add a few more comforts here and there, but there would be no substantial change in their spending habits or how they live their daily lives. And that is true of most people. If your portfolio jumped 50 percent, you probably wouldn't start wearing an ascot like Thurston Howell III from the old Gilligan's Island reruns and begin speaking in an affected nasal tone about your new yacht.

Now for another question: Would your life change significantly if you were to lose 50 percent of your portfolio? Most people say yes. Losing 50 percent of their life's savings would shake their financial foundations. They may immediately start cutting back on unnecessary expenses and become more conservative in nearly everything they did. Losing 50 percent of your portfolio could cause stress that would eventually affect your health. We know of married couples who had to seek counseling to repair their relationship when one of them is a more aggressive investor than the other. Things go along just fine until a market correction, and then the finger-pointing and the accusations begin. Money problems can cause serious problems between marriage partners. If such a thing occurs after a couple retires, instead of enjoying their "golden years" as they should, they spend their time worrying about money.

Core Mistakes Retirees Make

In the past quarter century, we have met with hundreds of retired folks and those who are approaching retirement, and we have made the observation that there is a commonality to the investing mistakes they tend to make. We find that most people don't understand how much risk they are assuming with their investments. That is why one of the first things we do in a *Retirement Roadmap Review®* process is a risk analysis. Since retirement represents a fundamental change in your life, it should follow that how we approach investing should shift fundamentally as well, but it often doesn't.

The most common mistake retirees make is investing as if they were still working. While we are working, we are our most valuable asset. Why? Because it is we who are producing the income. When we retire, we transfer that importance to our portfolio. It is now our portfolio, not we, who generates our paycheck. That's why we must treat our portfolio much differently in retirement than we did in those working years.

The second most common mistake is not taking proactive steps to protect their assets from significant drops in the market. Some investors have told us they felt powerless to prevent losses their portfolio. Because they didn't know what else to do, they watched like deer, frozen in the headlights of an oncoming tractor-trailer truck as their portfolios lost as much as half its value. In some cases, this happened multiple times, and they just took it as a matter of course, not knowing alternatives existed. Losing a significant portion of your portfolio is never easy, but it can be especially problematic during our retirement years when we have less time to earn it back.

Retirement Should Be a Worry-Free Zone

When we ask a roomful of people how they envision their retirement, we get a variety of answers that inevitably include such activities as golf, fishing, relaxing on beaches and playing with the grandkids. Not once do we ever hear someone tell us that they are looking forward to spending their retirement worrying about the stock market. No one wants to spend his or her retirement hunched over a computer screen, watching the ticker symbols flicker, or pacing the floor at night, wondering which way the market will go when the opening bell sounds the next morning. That is why a risk analysis is so crucial. When we ask the question, "What is your financial advisor doing to protect you from losses?" we often get a shrug of the shoulders or a blank look. That is because most "financial advisors" are either stockbrokers or insurance salespeople. They do not specialize in comprehensive, holistic retirement income planning.

Red flags should pop up if you ever hear the following from your financial advisor:

"Just hang in there and ride it out."

"Just sit tight and hold on; the market will come back."

"Don't feel like the Lone Ranger. Your losses weren't nearly as bad as some of my other clients."

And our personal favorite:

"Standard deviation analysis…what's that?"

Red flags should also pop up if you are encouraged to place all your assets in an annuity or any one single insurance product. Don't misunderstand us; there are many effective and useful financial products on the market, and we use many of them in presenting options to our clients every day. But there is no magic silver bullet or one-size-fits-all formula that can provide financial security and peace of mind in retirement. That only comes from a balanced approach that takes the entire retirement financial picture into consideration and combines the right investment strategies that fit your unique and individual situation.

No Panic Button Needed

You know your retirement income plan may be a bit on the risky side if it comes complete with a big red button that says, "PANIC" on it. One of the benefits of standard deviation analysis is providing individual risk tolerance and measuring sustainable losses. In fact, finding in each portfolio what is and what is not an acceptable loss is the basis for acceptable standard deviation. There are sustainable losses and unsustainable losses when it comes to your wealth, just like there are sustainable and unsustainable injuries when it comes to your health.

One fine spring afternoon, on a sunny day with the temperature in the 60s, Lori went into a ditch while riding her Harley-Davidson Softail Deluxe. It wasn't a good day for her. The bike landed on her, and she sustained three broken ribs and a sprained ankle. Besides her injured pride, that was the extent of it. She was a little sore, but the doctor said she would be okay. Those were sustainable injuries. The marks on her helmet told us that had she not been wearing it, she would probably have incurred unsustainable injuries — potentially life-threatening injuries — to her head.

In properly balancing your portfolio for appropriate risk, the job of a competent financial advisor is to help you determine where you are vulnerable, and to protect you from unsustainable losses while at the same time allowing for growth opportunities and guaranteed income that will enable you to enjoy a rich and fulfilling life for the rest of your retirement.

Ken and Lori Heise tackle Paris, summer 2018.

Selecting the Right Advisor For You

The last time we took a plane trip, the flight attendant came on the intercom just before we landed and instructed us to return our seat backs and tray tables to their full and upright position. Then she acknowledged that we had a choice when it came to air travel and thanked us for choosing Delta.

We hadn't really *chosen* Delta, of course. It just happened to be the airline that had a plane going to our destination at just the time we wanted to go. We didn't really care which airline took us there as long as we arrived safely. I'm sure most of the 200 or so people on the plane with us were like us. I doubt seriously if any of them made a list of all the airlines and compared their safety records. We take for granted that they are safe. Doesn't the Federal Aviation Administration regulate that sort of thing? Nor did any of us do research to rank prospective airlines according to schedule efficiency. Within reason, we expect them to get us there on time. We also didn't investigate which airline had the best and worst reputations for losing luggage. Quite frankly, flying anywhere is a bit of a hassle these days, no matter which carrier you use. As far as we were concerned, one airline was as good as another. Still, it was nice for the flight attendant to thank us for our business.

Is it any different when choosing a financial advisor? You bet it is! This is one decision that calls for care and due diligence on the part of anyone who is either retired or entering retirement. The state and federal government may regulate certain aspects of banking, investment and insurance but not who may claim the title "financial professional." Virtually anyone with the applicable license or registration can hang out a "financial professional" shingle or put that title under his or her name on a business card. Does that necessarily make them qualified to guide you in this critical phase of your financial life? Absolutely not!

Choose a specialist. As the title of this chapter suggests, the right financial advisor for one individual may not be right for another. The principle of different strokes for different folks applies here. Just as there are no two people who are exactly alike, no two financial situations are exactly alike either. There are (or there shouldn't be) any one-size-fits-all financial plans. Every situation is different. Two people can be the same age, earn identical incomes, have identical amounts of money in the bank and identical investments, but still require differing financial plans. Why? Because they are bound to have different uses in mind for their wealth. One wants to travel in retirement while the other wants to stay home and play with the grandchildren. One is legacy minded with an emphasis on charity while the other has no interest in either. It all depends on the individual. You want to select the right advisor for *you.*

There is just as much specialization in the financial profession as there is in the medical community. An adult will not seek treatment or care from a pediatrician. You likely won't go to a dentist for a heart problem. Likewise, if you are in the accumulation phase of your financial life (still working and

CHAPTER 11

building your nest egg) you want to work with a financial advisor who specializes in accumulation planning. On the other hand, if you are in the preservation and distribution phase of your financial life (retired and living on your savings) you need the services of a financial advisor who specializes in retirement income planning.

DIY not recommended. To continue with the medical metaphor, just as you wouldn't consider self-surgery or self-dentistry, we don't recommend the do-it-yourself approach to financial planning. Please don't misunderstand — we have clients who like to tinker with online trading accounts. That's not what we mean by do-it-yourself financial planning. Those folks are not placing their entire life's savings at risk. They enjoy following the stock market on their personal computers and enjoy researching their investments. The key is they use discretionary funds for this activity and do not build their financial plans around their investing hobby. That's perfectly alright. What we are discouraging is attempting to take on comprehensive financial planning by yourself. It takes a team of specialists to do it right. A competent financial advisory firm will be able to put together a team that may include any or all of the following: estate attorneys, elder care attorneys, tax planners, insurance specialists, money managers, real estate professionals, and the list goes on. That doesn't mean that when you meet with your financial advisor all of those people will be in the room, charging you by the hour for their expert help. It simply means that your advisor will be able to tap into the expertise of a number of professionals to help you meet your unique financial objectives.

In your search for a financial advisor who can provide strategies and products designed to provide you with a confident and successful retirement, places you probably won't find a candidate to fill that position include:

- **Family reunions**: Good old uncle George means well, but unless he has a background in finance, he is probably not the best source for financial advice.
- **The local coffee shop, neighborhood bar, or beauty salon**: Believe it or not, some have staked their financial future on conversations held or overheard at such places, often with disastrous results. Friends don't let friends take financial advice from office co-workers at the water cooler.
- **The internet**: It is true that you can find just about anything you are looking for on the internet, including financial advice. But for every expert opinion pointing north, you can find another one pointing south.
- **Your favorite bank teller**: The place where you bank may be very friendly and the people behind the counter may know you by your first name, but unless they are an Investment Advisor Representative or a Certified Financial Planner, they probably don't have the credentials or education to assist you with a comprehensive financial plan.

By the way, the above words of caution are reminiscent of those found printed in large letters above the emergency doors on airplanes: "Do Not Open While in Flight." That warning wouldn't be there if it weren't for the fact that at some point in the past someone attempted to do exactly that. We have heard horror stories of wrecked retirements because of well-meaning but untrustworthy advice volunteered by trusted but unqualified friends.

Ask lots of questions. The financial advisor you select works for you. Interview them just like you would if you were a business owner hiring a manager. You are looking for someone you can trust, someone with experience, training and proper credentials. But no matter how much education and certification your financial advisor candidate may have, it is critical that you are on the same page philosophically. You want your goals, your vision of the future, the purpose you have for your wealth imprinted on your financial plan. You do not want the financial advisor's agenda to dominate the end result. But what questions should you ask?

How are you paid? In polite society, asking someone how and how much they are compensated may be considered rude. In this case, however, it is business, not personal. You don't care about the financial professional's annual income. That's not the point. You are asking how he or she is compensated to determine if there is a possible conflict of interest. For example, Investment Advisor Representatives (IAR) usually work on a fee-only or a fee-plus-commissions basis. With fee-only compensation arrangements, the advisor charges either flat fees or hourly fees, somewhat like an attorney. Many IARs also charge you a fee equal to the percentage of the assets you have under management with them. Industry standards are usually between one-two percent. This rewards the advisor for growing your portfolio. The flat fees or hourly charges usually come with a one-time service, such as developing a financial plan or structuring an estate plan. The fee may vary according to the amount of service rendered or the size of the accounts involved. If the service includes the execution of stock market trades, the advisor will usually earn a commission for each trade the advisor makes on your behalf.

Commission is not a dirty word. Think of a travel agent. When you hire a travel agency to plan a trip for you, they try to (a) save you money on fares and hotel bills, and (b) enhance the efficiency and enjoyability of your trip. What does it cost you? Usually nothing! It is the business of the travel agent to find out where you are going, what you want to do there and how much is in your travel budget. Then the agent puts together the best fares, the best schedule and the best hotels for the best price and creates your itinerary. How is the travel agent compensated? By commissions from the vendors! Does it offend you that the hotels and airlines pay the agent a commission? It shouldn't. It doesn't come out of your pocket. In fact, if the travel agent is an expert it should put money *in* your pocket. If you had to do the work yourself, you might make a mess of it, and you would not likely possess the expertise to achieve the same results.

How do you approach investing? You might call this a "trick question." Why? Because if you ask it on the initial interview with your financial advisor candidate, a competent advisor will probably not give you an answer. Not right away, anyway. Why is that? Because the financial advisor's approach to investing should coincide with yours. How will the financial advisor candidate know what your approach to investing is until he or she asks you questions about such things as your risk tolerance, timetable, tax situation, estate plans, and income needs, and what your total financial picture looks like? Would you trust a doctor who prescribed medicine without first asking you about your allergies and what medication you were currently taking? I doubt it. The right advisor candidate for *you* will get to know *you* before recommending strategies.

Some who advertise their services as financial advisors are merely stockbrokers. One 61-year-old woman with whom we are acquainted told us that when she was looking for a financial advisor after the death of her husband, she visited the offices of a "financial advisory" firm and was disappointed. We asked her why and she told us that she had received a considerable death benefit from a life insurance policy and she wanted to know what to do with it. She recounted that the "financial advisors" gave here what amounted to a menu of three choices: risky, riskier and riskiest. She said that none of the "advisors" could provide her with a comprehensive retirement plan that guaranteed her a lifetime income. Instead, she was presented with colorful pie charts showing projected returns from various combinations of mutual funds, large cap stocks, small cap stocks, bonds and international stocks. They told her that her security lay in the fact that these investments were diversified.

"I was asking for a plan and they wanted only to sell me investments," she said.

This woman's case is not unusual. She was approaching retirement age and needed advice on when to take her Social Security, how to plan for possible long-term health care, and structuring her estate to avoid overpayment of taxes. She was talking to accumulation advisors, not preservation and distribution advisors. Investing is part of an overall financial plan, but it is only one piece of the puzzle.

Ask about credentials. True professionals will not mind if you ask them about their credentials, qualifications and certifications. They will not be insulted. Instead, they will be glad to tell you about the training they have received and proud to answer any questions you have about what qualifies them to advise you. You may find this information on the walls of their office or on their business card, although some are more modest than others in displaying this — another reason you may want to ask directly.

When you see those letters after the name of a financial advisor candidate on a business card, do they look like an alphabet scramble to you? If so, ask politely what they mean. The bearer of the card should be happy to answer you. There are nearly as many designations and certifications for financial advisors as there are letters in the alphabet, and not all are created equal.

Letters after one's name on a business card are just alphabet soup if they are not accompanied by education, training, experience, competence and — oh yes, that one factor that cannot be defined by plaques on the wall or letters on a business card — trustworthiness. All the education in the world cannot teach this character quality and there is no substitute for it. The best gauge for trustworthiness is how you feel about the individual or individuals you are interviewing. Sometimes you just know if the people on the other side of the table are responsible and accountable and will work in your best interests and not their own. The bond of trust is something you both build with each other over time.

Are you a fiduciary? We covered this in chapter three, but it bears repeating. A fiduciary (a word which means true) is a legal standard for a professional who is sworn to act in your best interests regardless of any other personal considerations. A fiduciary is ethically, morally and legally bound to offer you advice that promotes your financial well-being and not that of his or her own. If you ask that question and you get a blank stare, or if you have to explain the definition, start looking for the exit door — you're in the wrong place.

How will we work together long-term? You simply must have good communication with your advisor. Who will your designated contact person be when you call the office to ask a question? Will you have access to the firm's principals in the future if you need them? How often will your financial plan be reviewed? Who are the other members of your professional team? What role do each of them play?

Your advisor should review your financial plan with you at least once a year. Tax rules change. Government guidelines change. Last year's strategies may not be the best for this year's economic climate.

Finally, remember that it is not about the advisor, it is about *you*. The advisor is your financial guide on your retirement journey, but ultimately it is your journey and you are the only one who can legitimately be in charge of it. You are captain of your ship and your financial advisor is merely your navigator whose job it is to help you avoid the dangers and enjoy the joys of your retirement journey.

About the Authors

Ken and Lori Heise live and work in the St. Louis area. With a combined 50-plus years' experience as financial professionals behind them, the couple founded Heise Advisory Group in 2006. Shortly after, they were married, and have enjoyed working together ever since, helping their clients plan for a successful retirement future.

Ken, who serves as president of Heise Advisory Group, is an Investment Advisor Representative as well as a Registered Financial Consultant. He is also a Top of the Table member of the Million Dollar Round Table, placing him among the elite of financial and insurance professionals worldwide.[15]

Ken considers it his personal mission to give clients confidence about their finances and help them make informed decisions so

---

[15] Million Dollar Round Table ("MDRT") is a membership organization. Qualifying criteria for membership include attaining specified levels of commissions earned, premium paid or income earned on the sale of insurance and other financial products. The MDRT membership requires the payment of annual dues, compliance with ethical standards, and to be in good standing with an MDRT-approved Professional Association. There are 3 levels of membership which include standard membership, Court of the Table and Top of the Table. The MDRT logo and/or trademarks are property of their respective owners and no endorsement of Ken or Lori Heise or Heise Advisory Group is stated or implied.

they can live their retirement years to the fullest. "This is a responsibility I take very seriously," Ken says, "and I treat every client as if they were my own mother or father. I am dedicated to building warm, friendly relationships with our clients and taking a sincere interest in their values, plans, and dreams for the future."

When it comes down to it, Lori's true passion is people. In 1989, she found a way to translate that passion into a career in the insurance industry. Lori is a licensed insurance professional and specializes in helping clients preserve their assets and provide guaranteed lifetime incomes based on individual client needs. Lori enjoys exercise, travel and, most of all, spending time with her family.

Lori considers it her personal mission to strive to be a better person each day and bring happiness to others through her compassion, sense of humor, and kindness.

"I believe that all good things are achieved through hard work, integrity, honesty and a commitment to excellence," she says. "Just having the opportunity to sit down every day with new people and learn about them — who they are and where they want to be — that is what motivates me. I'm grateful to do what I love, to help people achieve their financial goals, to help take a little of that burden from them."

Personal and Professional History

Lori grew up in St. Louis, Missouri, while Ken grew up in Milwaukee, Wisconsin. Ken began his career as a financial professional in 1990 representing Aid Association for Lutherans, a company which specialized in mutual funds, annuities and life insurance. In 2003, he passed the Series 65 and Series 7 exams. After spending some time with New York Life, he established his own financial advisory firm.

Meanwhile, Lori's career began in 1989 when she began selling life and health insurance. While Ken's career path led him farther down the road of money management and investment counseling, Lori continued to gain greater expertise in the insurance field. Their paths merged in 2005 when they met at a business conference. They decided to make St. Louis their home and in 2006 founded Heise Advisory Group. They were married in 2007. Lori, who serves as vice president of the firm, specializes in the insurance side of the business, and Ken handles the investment side.

When Ken and Lori met, conversation came easily because they both shared a love for riding motorcycles. Their passion for serving the financial needs of their clients is matched only by their love of riding their Harley Davidsons when their work schedules permit. Vacation to them translates to adventures spent exploring the blue highways on a map of America. They have visited many states on their Harleys and would eventually like to see them all.

Family is extremely important to Ken and Lori. They have four adult children — Rachel, Becky, Malia and Sam—and four grandchildren to spoil — Hayden, Gabriella, Katie and Mollie. They also like to consider their clients as members of their "extended family" and sponsor several client appreciation social events throughout the year.

"Even though Heise Advisory Group has grown quite large since we started, we still maintain quality family-like relationships with all of our valued clients," says Ken.

The Heises place a great emphasis on education for retirees and those on the threshold of retirement. In addition to the retirement seminars they sponsor, Ken and Lori jointly host a weekly radio show where they answer questions posed by listeners about the financial side of retirement.

"Working together as a husband and wife team gives our clients something unique and special," says Lori. "Ken is a numbers person and I love working with people. Ken excels at listening to people and understanding their financial goals and I love working with him to put the numbers together to help people achieve their dreams."

"When it comes to motorcycles, it's all about the journey — a chance to get out and see this great country of ours," says Ken.

"As we ride through the open country and the back roads of the United States, we get the sense that nothing is restricted; everything is open and free and we have not a care in the world," adds Lori. "And that's how I envision retirement. Life is a journey. Every day is a journey."

Lori, Ken, son Sam and daughter-in-law Kelsey, join Lori's brother's family in a photo before Lori heads to donate a kidney to her niece (middle).

Acknowledgments

At the time of writing this book, we have been in the financial industry for nearly 30 years. We have always wanted to write a book to help others through the retirement journey. Why has it taken so long for us to write this book?

Well, a life that included raising our four children, starting our own company and more importantly, helping individual families make the transition from their working years to retirement and beyond. Though we wanted to write this book for a long time, we could not do so at the expense of family, or by taking time away from our clients and the company that we so love.

How did we find the time now? Well, it has taken many adjustments. Our children have grown and moved into their own careers and families and our amazing office team that works seamlessly to provide service and support to our clients has given us more free time to get the project completed.

The idea of this book comes from years of meeting with individual families that were unprepared and needing guidance.

Why would anyone be interested in what we have to say? Good question! The answer provides the foundation for this book. People crave information and they want unbiased, honest advice and opinions on what they can do with their money. We all have three major priorities in common: our families, our health and our money., with the latter being something we can speak to. This book is filled with years of experience that we are excited to share.

We can safely say that all this would not be possible without the utmost love and support we have for each other and our family. Thank you to our children, Rachel, Becky, Malia and Sam! Your love, support and encouragement have been an endless source of motivation and has given us the confidence to put our thoughts into words to make this book possible.

Thank you to all of our staff at Heise Advisory Group, both past and present. Without your unwavering commitment to our company and our clients, this would not be possible. Thank you to our editor Tom Bowen for all the time and dedication in helping us craft our story. Lastly, thank you to Regina Stephenson for the final push to pull everything together to get this project complete and published. This has been a labor of love, a team effort, and we could not have completed this project without all of you.

The Heises celebrate the 2016 wedding of daughter Malia. From left: daughter Malia and son-in-law Nick, granddaughter Katie, granddaughter Mollie, Lori and Ken, grandson Hayden, daughter Becky, daughter Rachel, daughter-in-law Kelsey and son Sam.

Made in the USA
Lexington, KY
11 November 2018